Living on the Edge of Heaven

G. Edward

Copyright © 2017 G. Edward

All rights reserved.

ISBN-13: 978-0-9988366-0-7
ISBN-10: 9988366-0-5:

"There's more to a moment than you know. Make them count."
The Author

Table of Contents

Introduction i

A Little Soul 1

The Iowa Wedding 3

Squirrels 9

Magic 17

The Edge of Heaven 25

Over the Edge 27

Sister Meredith 29

Purpose 39

Dreams 41

Janice 43

Every Blessed Day 49

Jane 53

Love and War 59

Free Will 65

Hills 69

The Road 75

Fear 81

The Cistern 85

Grandma 93

Uncle Ted 97

His Will be Done 103

Dust Motes 105

Bits of Dust 107

Big Carp 111

Educational Opportunities 121

Lead My Sheep 133

Dad's Tractor 139

Pie 145

Clues 149

Sixteen 151

Act 157

Racoon Riches 161

Monte Carlo 167

It's Complicated 175

Good Luck 177

The Last Year 193

A Moment *199*

Dad Goes Home 201

INTRODUCTION:

Have you met your soul? Do you know your purpose, the reason for this great adventure on earth? How do the comic, tragic, arduous yet mundane hours of our lives reflect God's plan? Follow a boy and his soul as they experience such a journey and come to know each other.

The story begins as God creates our little soul and whispers His plans before setting him upon the earth. Like boys everywhere, he is unaware of God's presence, yet remains curious of how the world works, how people behave, and what his part to play might be. While sleeping, our little boy's soul can rest at the edge of heaven and meet with God to discuss the great questions life presents.

As he grows, life becomes more complex, the questions harder, yet the answers make more sense.

A Little Soul

The little soul became aware and felt the warmth of God. "My young soul! I'll give you a moment to absorb all you can!" and God chuckled. He always loved this part when He made another new soul. "I have plans for you," he assured the little soul with love and joy and purpose.

The young soul harnessed his awareness. He already knew many things. Indeed, he was in the presence of God having been made of God. But he sensed something remote. Something he was not part of, and he knew it was eternal ecstasy.

"You will come back for that, my young soul. First you will make a grand adventure. While heaven is miraculous, it is made better by the adventures of souls who return. You are going to the physical realm. During your adventure will come surprises, tests, and challenges. While awake, your senses will be dimmed, your physical body will not hear me, or see me. I do this so you can learn from fresh experience." The little soul longed for the heaven he could feel beyond his reach.

He asked, "Is this necessary?"

And God continued, "Ecstasy wants for pain to recognize itself. Love must be given to be experienced. Wisdom grows not from within, but without. You, My young soul, are amongst the billions of souls I made, to bring back their adventure for all in heaven to share. When returning, you may experience the adventures from every soul of all time. From their pain, work, and love you will know the joy that is heaven."

The young soul standing in God's presence wondered, "What is my purpose on this adventure?"

"Insightful question. I did OK with you! You understand the adventure itself is the purpose. You also sense as you now exist separate of Me you are unique. Your journey will be yours with its own purpose. I said I had plans for you, yes?" The young soul was told the ubiquity of his physical body would keep his daily awareness from understanding his purpose for many years. But his soul would remember what his body could not and guide him back to his path when necessary. "Your choices will be your own, or perhaps for others to make as you allow. Your adventure will mingle with those of many others."

"And if I am lost?"

"We will talk sometimes when your body is sleeping. As your body rests, you can find respite here at the edge of heaven. You'll rarely remember your dreams, but I will be with you always. If you find Me from the awareness of your body, you may be confused. To understand Me is beyond the need. Many souls have discovered an element of Me and became both pious and manic, genius and prolific. They created and brought wondrous moments to the physical world. I can assure you your choices will have results you cannot predict. It is a grand adventure.

You will soon begin. Let's look there in a place called Iowa. A young couple is taking their wedding vows. They are making plans for you. Your future uncle Ted is arriving. Do you see his wife, Loretta next to him? The whole family is coming. Let's watch, and then you'll be on your way."

The Iowa Wedding

From a large extended family, the wedding is an event happening once or twice a year. A timeless event each generation repeats. One cannot tell what year it is, 1960, 1990, 2020? The ritual is perfected in every detail that matters.

This wedding is in a town much the same as others. A collection of homes built out from the center a decade at a time. A few century homes behind main street with revival or Victorian attempts. American Four-squares lined the original streets laid down with determination in straight lines. More modest bungalows surround them. Was that a Sears kit home? The ranch style neighborhoods once sat at their edge of town. Someone sampled a Frank Lloyd Wright idea. Practical colonials and an occasional original farmhouse are found by the new school at the new edge of town.

The towns in this part of Iowa have a church, and while it is either Catholic, or Lutheran, the men who built the church were German immigrants. The churches hold perhaps forty large families that still sit in the high straight-backed wooden pews. The elongated stained glass windows stretch to an arched point. The altar is gilded. A center aisle, and two side aisles offer public or more private places to worship. If one falls asleep in church, you will wake up wondering what town, and what church you are in. You check for kneelers to know which kind of service it will be.

Ted and Loretta enter and a gangly young usher sporting his first tux obediently takes the lady's arm.

"Groom's family" she informs him, and he marches her up the aisle. Ted has learned to go easy and trail him about six extra steps. Our young usher is likely to reach the pew, try to unwind his arm, and spin around to get out of there as fast as he can. Too close and the collision is unavoidable. Plopped in the midst of family, the air in church is awake with excitement. The adults are talking in church like kids on Sunday shouldn't.

The church is filled to a point that would make a Sunday proud. Up in the fourth pew a hand pops up and begins a frantic dance. The hand shouts a whisper to the back of the church, "Nancy! Up here! Oh look, Nancy made it! Nancy, up heeeere!!!" Somehow, Nancy hears the whisper from the very back of the church and no one else notices. Nancy scurries up the aisle, and it is clear she's not a local anymore. The painted-on tube dress, a dark tan, bleached hair, and her, um... shoes are definitely not real.

The promenade begins with the ushers seating the grandparents. The grandmas are sporting new pant suits in fresh spring colors that will clash in the pictures. At this wedding the grandpas are gone, but if the grandpas make it, they will wear suits that pre-date the birth of the couple. The grandpas are invisible at these events, whether they are there or not, and they know it.

The parents are brought forward. The mothers are wearing hair styles and dresses they've never worn before or will again. Pictures will record for posterity the mothers looking like people no one ever knew. The dads are trailing the ushers by about six paces, and would be invisible like the grandpas, except they get to wear the tux.

Bach, played from a real organ, beckons the wedding party to step forward. The bridesmaids wear dresses chosen to make the bride look good. If you happen to know any of the groomsmen, you are taken aback by how well they clean up. A ring bearer and flower girl are next, and one is always too young, and the other does a good job hauling them from one end of the aisle to the other. Everyone smiles.

The bride is young, and the dress is unique, but also the same in the way that young ladies try to be unique but the same as their friends. A wedding march is played, and she pulls it off with smiles. Hugs and handshakes up front, and then, oh, yeah... there's the groom. He's already getting that invisible thing figured out.

We hear the readings, Abraham was how old? Men love your wives, and the best wine at the wedding came last. Minds wander or perhaps meditate, it's hard to tell. Stand up, sit down, and wake up, we've got the couple standing up front now. The most feared tragedies don't happen. The rings are there, no one steps on the dress, the vows are said, the parson does not crack a joke.

The vestibule of these churches will not hold the receiving line, so it goes outside. It's a warm windy day so the ladies are holding their skirts down, and the little girls are letting them fly. The expensive hairdo's have done their job, so it's over. At this point the couple gets to do something unique in how they leave. An interesting car, a carriage, a tandem bike, or heck let's just walk, the reception is only five blocks. Everyone else drives.

The reception is at the local American

Legion/VFW/women's auxiliary hall, which rents for the price of tap beer for the night. Out front we find a memorial for the local boys who died. A weathered bronze plaque for the boys who served in THE world war guards the door. More plaques for all the wars that followed form a line. Pictures of the local kids currently in the service hang just inside, and we look for the ones we recognize so we can ask their families how they are doing.

The two clans organize themselves around tables on opposite sides of the room. You can smell the food. It is Iowa, so pork and beef will be served. A couple of sisters or aunts are buzzing around making sure everything is right. This is their part of the event. One has a baby on the hip, and her free hand is waving and pointing while she gives instructions to a couple of ten-year-old boys. They are wearing a fresh set of church clothes, a couple sizes too large, that they are expected to grow in to.

As the extended family collects around tables for dinner, someone has brought a date and the hazing of an outsider begins. The women are nice, but watch carefully. The guys are crude and cruel and funny and the women apologize for them and watch even closer.

The maid of honor and best man make toasts, which are poignant and well done, and we are surprised. The bar opens and there are two choices for beer, a national brand and its light version. It's not very good until the third one, after which even the bridesmaids are looking better. After another people remember how to dance! Perhaps one more for courage as there will be a polka somewhere in the set.

The couple and wedding party dance and then

the night gets down to business. A mix of pieces to please every generation is played. The twenty-somethings are at the bar acting like adults, and the adults are on the dance floor acting like kids. Once the chicken dance and hokey pokey are accomplished, the farmers with livestock to feed can leave. The older folks can leave because the music is soon going to hell.

It's time for the Electric Slide and the Macarena and maybe a line dance. The livestock widows and everyone who is single for every reason take the floor. Flushed and ready they find reluctant dance partners. Shoes come off, and fifty pairs of pantyhose are ruined after one use. Two tunes short of a heart attack a slow song comes along for those who want to sway with their sweetheart. Someone is asking for a date. Someone is asking for more. Someone must plan the next wedding just like this.

The time comes for the bride to throw her bouquet. The least likely bridesmaid lunges for it. This great traditional sign from the universe might be her only hope. The desperate group knocks over a ten-year-old who bounces off the dance floor like a rubber ball and reaches up to see the bouquet.

The garter is removed and tossed. The single guys step back to let a gaggle of six-year-olds wrestle on the floor for it. Everyone smiles.

The hairdos are gone, clothing is rumpled and torn, the makeup smeared, but the hall is dim. Daylight betrays all so most don't leave until dark. And on the way home weddings are planned and remembered. Babies are planned and remembered. A glimmer in the eye that night. There will be more Iowa weddings.

Squirrels

Life on a farm in Iowa isn't heaven. It's not the edge of heaven. Perhaps it's the first step off the edge. Farmers work the four seasons to create the daily bread. Neighbors practice the golden rule and help before being asked. Kids can run but respect the grownups when a sharp word seems necessary. The questions, struggles and cruelty of life are still dispatched, but heaven is nearby. Farmers depend on God's grace and their own hard work. A trip to the country is a dip in cool water. There are storms to ride if you stay.

Whilst one prays and works, the farm is shared with abundant life. In the tradition of farmers who settled the prairie, life on our farm was productive. Trees bore fruit or nuts. They blocked the wind, became lumber, and grew to be firewood. Crops and gardens bore sustenance. The few flowers raised could decorate the church or be placed upon graves. Chickens laid, cows milked, sheep were sheared, and pigs were committed to breakfast. Cats moused, and dogs protected us from the night. Dogs were special. Glad to see you, ready to play, ready to eat, ready to nap. They were loyal sentries.

Yes, life was productive. Except for the critters. The natural wilderness was lurking, trying to take back the farm. There were the weedy shoots crawling from beneath the ground. Strangling young plants and sucking away their moisture. The bugs invaded from alien lands to infest livestock and consume plants. The prairie wanted the farm back. While it fought the crops and livestock with weeds and bugs, it reserved its shock troops to scare the people off the land.

Critters arrived by land, sea, and air. It was best to go inside at night as the critters could see in the dark. We knew they were coordinating attacks as we listened to coyotes and owls transmitting messages. The Morse code of crickets directed the front lines. All quiet meant danger. Rapid chirps, all clear, advance! Night attacks were yielded to the critters. The dogs would engage, and we listened to the fierce battles from behind the screens of our bedroom window. On a good night, the increasing distance of the barks told us the dogs had succeeded in chasing the critters away. On other nights, there were yelps and snarls and wounds to dress in the morning. Sometimes a terrible stench came from a nocturnal battle, and we had the choice of sleeping with the smell or closing the windows and sweating it out. In the daylight, we had a chance.

My younger brother Stevie and I ventured into fine summer mornings helping dad with chores. Our young legs ran to keep up with his long strides. Feeding and watering chickens, one moment dad would be handling birds and eggs, the next moment he would be off running and stomping. “Gol darn critters eating all the chicken feed. Gotta get the cats back in here.” Cats were a main line of defense against small critters. Expected to hold their own, cats were fed once a day and made up the rest by feasting on the goblins of the prairie.

One sunny morning, as dad had chores well under control, Stevie and I wandered off for our daily discoveries. Never disappointed, we came upon a fight scene from the previous night.

"What do you suppose it was?" Stevie was poking the remains with a stick.

"I'll bet it was a mountain lion."

"But the fur is all black and white."

"Probably a puma. Maybe an old one going grey. Skip and Sherman sure put up quite a fight last night." Skip and Sherman were the farm dogs. A genetic mix of most of the dogs in the area, they were products of the farm, and dedicated to its survival."

"Skip and Sherman do a good job. And the cats do too."

"Yeah, but you know, there's one set of critters the cats and dogs never get. The squirrels." Iowa farm-raised fox squirrels. Twice as large as gray squirrels, the fox squirrel has a burnt red coat with bellies in shades of tan. Athletic, they can run the vertical causeway of trunks and branches, and jump across wind-blown tree tops. If they miss, and fall fifty feet, they will bounce and climb the closest trunk with scant recognition their vertical detour occurred at all. But most of all, according to dad, fox squirrels ate a bushel-a-day of corn. They would starve the animals and then us as well. An occasional meal of fox squirrel tasted mighty good to dad.

The fox squirrels were faster than the cats, and would climb turn and scold the dogs for upsetting their day. While the dogs did their best to tree the squirrels, the squirrels bounced across the top of the farm with dashes across open ground to corn cribs, barns, or feed troughs. The dogs couldn't be everywhere. We were defenseless against squirrels.

Stevie and I resolved to battle the squirrels. It was our duty.

In any great declaration of war, early engagements reveal hard truths. We had things yet to learn. Our young calculating minds determined the corn crib was a giant squirrel lure. The crib was a small barn with an open latticework for sides. There was an open center so wagons could be pulled through for loading. With a wood shingle roof and open breezy sides, the corn could dry and keep for years. Dad had built screens throughout the insides of the crib to stop squirrels from setting up permanent residence. The snakes living under the shed kept the mice under control.

Set in an open spot easy for wagons to pull alongside, squirrels would have to make a dash across the open ground to climb the sides. Unable to penetrate dad's screens, they had to cling to the sides and chew on the exposed grain. While they could cling to a high side and ignore the dogs, they would be easy prey for us. Armed with BB guns and dried clay dirt clods we approached the corn crib through its long morning shadow. Circling to its sunny side we peeked around the corner. There! Three giant fox squirrels munching away at our livelihood! We flanked the enemy with a rush, launching our dirt clods. We fired BB's, and cranked our little lever actions for more shots on the run.

The squirrels, caught by surprise, ran around the sides of the crib. As they rounded each corner, they stopped and waited for us to come around before scampering around the next. They teased us for laps around the crib like a track coach getting his team in shape. After burning off breakfast, Stevie and I lay on a sunny pile of spilt corn to catch our breath. It was clear tactics would have to change. "Hey, they always circle the crib running away from us," I said. "Why don't you walk around this side, and I'll circle the other way. We'll trap them in the middle." Sam Houston would have chuckled at our plan. Breaking with convention, we divided our forces and encroached from two sides. The trap was sprung as we bolted from two corners of the crib, launching again with dirt grenades and BBs. Trapped and surprised, two squirrels went to the roof, while the young one panicked and went to the ground.

We chased the little guy on the ground across the yard, as he beat a retreat for a tree at the corner of the animal barn. Just then, Sherman trotted around the edge of the barn to come upon two boys and a squirrel running toward him. Upon Sherman engaging his legs, the squirrel noticed the heavy artillery moving at his front. Squirrels are smart. This squirrel, calculating he was hopelessly surrounded, decided his fate was best served by taking down the weaker of the enemy forces. The squirrel turned and mounted a high-speed attack at Stevie and me. Now, with momentum of the battle shifting, it was our turn to run. We made a line for the corn crib and circled, hoping the squirrel would choose a safe retreat up the side, rather than face the certain death of engaging us and Sherman in battle.

In the fog of war, battle lines change moment by moment. Sherman's barking had aroused reinforcements, and Skip appeared on the scene. Just as the squirrel could have decided to either engage

Stevie and I in battle, or turn to the safety of the corn crib, Skip cut off their option, and forced an encirclement and battle. With adrenaline heightening our logical abilities, Stevie and I decided to lure the squirrel away from the safety of the corn crib and back into the open. We ran.

Skip and Sherman pressed the attack barking like canons, and the squirrel once again turned to attack the lesser force and came right at us. Now it was Stevie and I running for the tree at the edge of the barn. With clear logic, we knew the tree offered sanctuary to the squirrel, so we would cut off its escape route, and let Skip and Sherman finish the job. Up the tree we went. Still learning from our first battlefield engagement, we found that squirrels are ruthless enemies. He pressed the attack right up the tree. Having dropped our guns to climb we were out-gunned facing the enemy in close quarters. Without defensive options, we maneuvered to a limb and dropped to the roof of the barn.

We breathed a hard minute as the squirrel called off his suicide attack, and sat in the upper branches, scolding the dogs. “Hey, with us on the barn, and Skip and Sherman on the ground, we have him surrounded. All we need to do is starve him out.” The siege lines were drawn. But the squirrel was better fed than us, and it was our bellies starving before his. Skip and Sherman kept up the fight for a while. Later, while sitting in the kitchen eating grilled cheese sandwiches we saw the squirrel hop to the barn roof, run across the top and down the opposite side. A few short leaps across the lawn, and he was running a course across the top of the orchard, impervious, aloof, effortless.

"Darn critters." Dad was right. A breeze tossed the apple trees enough to see green fruit. Chickens clucked. The sheep and calves milled in the yard. We could smell corn pollen. Life was productive. But lurking, always lurking...

Magic

Stevie came along a year after my grand entrance. We were raised as two calves in the same pen. Same room, same food, same clothes, same swimming lessons. By the time we started grade school we were the same size. I was a full grade ahead, and a full year older, making me the brains of the operation. That worked out well as Stevie always had questions. So much to learn, so little time.

There were long stretches of childhood where Stevie and I were constant companions. While we had the run of the orchard, garden, and farm, neighbors were a bit spread out. Opportunities to play with neighbor kids were frequent enough, but tended to be scheduled by the moms. If our personal assistants were not considering how to schedule our daily play time, it was up to us to roam around and find things to do. "What appointments are on the agenda today?" I might ask.

"Get outside, I'm canning beans," and our day would be under way. A magnificent world of wonder just outside the door.

Stevie was lucky to have a superior intellectual mentor at his disposal. He made good use of our time together, continually asking questions. I admit I learned from the experience as well. If you are put in a position where someone asks a question, then it is an obligation to provide an answer. While Stevie would ask questions that never occurred to me, I was pressured to deliver a reasonable answer. I learned a lot of things from the answers I came up with.

A line of questions would often lead to an experiment or two. “What is dirt? Why do worms eat dirt? Can we eat dirt?” We engaged in self-directed scholarship. “Do worms live in mud? Does mud taste like dirt?” The laboratory was well stocked and ready. “Can we make dirt? Dad says manure turns into dirt. Why do the worms like the manure better than the dirt?” The lack of prior life experience allowed us to explore questions in unorthodox ways. “Why does the chicken crap smell worse than the cow poop? What kind of dirt happens if you mix the two? Do you need mud to mix stuff up to make dirt?” But like many genius scientists, our unconventional approaches got rejected by academics.

“My God boys! What have you been doing? Geeze, you will NOT come in the house. I am hosing you down and you are taking those clothes off and going straight into the bath tub.” Same tub, same cocoa and toast, same bedtime.

We were sitting at the top of the hill in the tall grass one hot summer afternoon. The wind was forcing undulating waves through the ripe brome heads, and the dry surf would roll up and brush our faces again and again. It was warm and, thunderstorms were boiling up in the west. You could see lightning in the clouds. “I see an alligator head!”

“I see it, hey look, that’s a giant slug.” The clouds boiled and changed and crept up on us, promising cooler weather behind them.

“What’s electricity?” Stevie asked. I was renown throughout the neighborhood for my electrical accidents and considered an expert on the topic. Electric fences offered free access to dozens of experiments involving electricity. Bare light bulbs dangling in the barn, and their empty sockets, made for hours of fun, and sometimes fires.

A question was posed; therefore, I would soon add to our education. An answer had to be formed, and this one needed to be good. Electricity was complicated after all. "You know the power plant down by the river? They have big coils of wire in there. They have big tubes reaching up into the sky, and the electricity come down from the sky through the tubes. And they have a big fire inside. When they cook the big wire coils the electricity goes into the wires. And then they connect all the power lines from the houses back to the power plant to suck off the electricity." There, that was pretty good, I thought.

"Well everyone knows that, but what is the electricity?" Stevie was stretching for graduate level answers. This was deep water, and I was in over my head. I had felt the shocks, the burns, the jolts. I had scars. This was a subject in which I had genuine experience. And yet, it was a real head scratcher.

"The electricity is magic. You see, clouds get really high like those over there, and brush up against heaven. Some of the magic in heaven gets scraped off. You can see it in the lightning. That's a little bit of magic from heaven. Heaven's magic is so strong it jumps down through the clouds as lightning bolts. So the electricity left over is floating around in the sky, and the guys at the power plant are sucking it into the wires so we can use it." Now that was an answer from God. My performance in catechism class would prevent a career track to the papacy. However, understanding practical divine intervention was not limited to the Holy See.

"I think I want to be an electrician," Stevie mused.

On another day, perched atop another hill, the deep reflection upon mysterious things continued. We had been rolling things down the hill. A particularly steep part of the farm, left to grow rough as neither machinery nor adults could traverse the face of such a grade. Young boys, dogs, and spiders seemed to do fine. In the academic halls of Newtonian physics, this was another grand laboratory. All types of devices could be positioned at the precipice, nudged, and then examined during the careening descent and ultimate crash. The re-discovery of levers, pulleys, and forced labor from neighbor kids occurred during recovery and ascent operations. Investigations included hydraulics and hydrology. When all of mom's garden hoses were put together they would just reach from the spigot to the top of the hill. Besides the natural architectural power of water eroding soil on its downhill journey, we studied how to harness water with dams, channels, and terraces. Altering friction was a colossal discovery as wet grass made slippery slopes. The hill was a physics lab worthy of merit and coaxed higher order questions out of Stevie.

"Why do things fall down? I mean why don't they just go sideways or up?" Now we had been observing this phenomenon for days. Yet he had an excellent question. Dry, wet, round, or shaped like a bicycle, things always went down.

"It's magic."

"Like electricity?"

"Yes, but a different kind of magic. You see, God

put magic in the earth to hold everything down. If he didn't, everything would just go up to heaven, and nobody would stay down here. So the magic in the earth pulls everything down and keeps it out of heaven."

"How do we go to heaven?" The follow-up questions were often more difficult.

"Remember when they buried Grandpa in the cemetery? They put him in a box in the ground. Someday God will turn off the magic, and everything will get to fall up to heaven, even from the cemetery." The Priesthood was an option, but the nuns thought I had behavior problems, so maybe not.

After a year or two, formal education kicked in. I don't remember the grade it happened, but it occurred to me they were trying to teach us stuff. I think it was the day Miss Ripker gave us a special lesson. The school was chock full of students with no rooms to put them. A damp chamber in a basement corner of the old brick schoolhouse was pressed in to service as Miss Ripker's classroom. Miss Ripker was drawn straight from the pages of Hansel and Gretel. The witch, of course. Really old, like most adults. Ugly enough to scare birds away, which explained why she had never married.

We cooked "stone soup" one day while we read the story by the same title. The story was about a traveling shyster who talked people into making his stone soup. He "just" needed a pot of water, and he provided the stone. As the story progressed, he wheedled out of his benefactors the ingredients for a grand vegetable stew. Learning how to manipulate people was interesting enough, but Miss Ripker thought there was more to the story.

Miss Ripker's acting out of the old fable played like a dark tale. She enjoyed boiling up a great brew in a giant kettle perched on a tiny electric burner in the middle of the classroom. Each child would read a section of the story and walk up to deposit an ingredient. Miss Ripker's excitement grew as each child read another part of the spell and delivered another ingredient. The cackling was hard on the ears after a while. Somehow, we learned something.

"Class, today we must talk about something serious. This school has a fallout shelter, and we must learn how to use it. Someday, the Russians may fly over and drop atomic bombs on us, unless we get to them first. We will need to go into our shelter to survive. Now watch this movie about atomic bombs."

I expect the movie was intended to get our full cooperation. It was an awesome movie. It explained how scientists had figured out that the whole world and even the people were made of little bitty parts called atoms. Atoms were small, but really strong, and if you broke them apart, kapow! See ya later, Cincinnati.

The boys loved the movie. The girls looked pale and scared. One of them was crying because she had peed her pants. Miss Ripker pressed on. She was very serious about the atomic threat. "OK class, if the sirens blow, we need to go to our fallout shelter. There we will have food and water stored up for many days until it is safe to come out. We will practice getting in line and going to our assigned place in the shelter. In a real emergency, if there isn't time to get to the shelter, we will get under our desks. Aren't you glad we have a classroom in the basement?"

I got home and had to tell Stevie about the atomic threat movie. At some point, Stevie interrupted me, "Why is there so much energy in the atoms?" And it was another good question. Up to that point, I just thought it was cool that every atom inside a person had enough energy to wipe out a city. But that did seem like a lot of wasted energy, just to hold someone together. The nuclear force was a serious stumper, so I drew from the deep well of custom knowledge.

"You know, it's got to be another magic force. There's no way you can just grow a baby with that much energy inside by feeding it bananas and soup. The nuclear force just has to be magic from God."

Years passed, and I went to college to study mechanical engineering and Stevie went to study electrical engineering. The first day of freshman physics, Dr. Delfer paced in front of the class. "This is physics. We study the laws of nature, the forces of the universe." He rubbed his hands, excited about teaching a new class of freshmen. He looked over the top of his rimless spectacles, "You know what we are talking about is magic!" I sat up a little higher in the chair. "We can measure the electro-magnetic force, harness it into materials, predict what it will do, and create all kinds of wonderful devices. But the electro-magnetic force is invisible, without form, intangible. Now gravity is a force between all masses in the universe. While we can measure it, apply it to good use, predict its behavior, it also remains invisible, massless, formless, and beyond our senses. We will also learn about the strong and the weak forces, the nuclear forces." Beginning a crescendo, "Atoms have negatively charged electron shells, and positively charged protons clustered in the center. It's beyond reason why these atoms stay together, violating what we think we know about the magnetic force. If we release this force, we discover awesome amounts of energy changing form, rapidly and destructively!" At this point he delivered a dramatic pause, smiled and went on. "The nuclear force is not only invisible and massless, but resides within every cell in our bodies. The work of physicists has not ended as the great forces of the universe still present us with curious and unexplained problems. In the old days, people called that magic!"

The Edge of Heaven

The little soul was sitting at the edge of heaven when God appeared. "Enjoying the view?"

"Yes God. A beautiful creation. I was just thinking about how you created perfection from the smallest elements, to the vast universe. You made a place for us, and gave us bodies, and set us upon a purpose. But there I am today scaring the chickens by tossing firecrackers at them. How can I even do Your work? I am so far from You."

God chuckled, "You had those hens flying! Reminds me of the day your dad tried to harness cats to pull a sled. Now that was funny. The cats didn't much go for his harness, but he worked so hard!"

"But what about the big stuff? What about the world and creation?"

"First, remember, I've got that. Then also remember, the physical universe is just dust. Whether a mountain or tree or your body, all that dust is interesting, but it never had much imagination. As you create your gift for Me, it will come from the intangible. Don't cut down trees and move rocks and build monuments to show others you love Me. When I bring you home your dust will be left behind. Instead, bring me something interesting! What you thought, who you helped, experiences you had, how you felt, what you did. Share your gifts with others. Go face fear and create joy. And, scare a few chickens now and then. If you make me laugh that's good, too!"

Over the Edge

Stevie and I were eating breakfast. The school bus would soon squeal to a stop by our mailbox. Mom taught first grade now at a Catholic school. She went to work in case Dad died so we wouldn't starve to death. A strapping forty-year-old vision of health, dad worked a farm and had a job book-keeping for Texaco at the pipe line. All was well, yet the persistent worry of imminent disaster made perfect sense somehow. Disaster would strike, just a matter of when. Enjoy breakfast every day while you can.

We enjoyed our Cocoa Puffs, a breakfast in under a minute. Mom was percolating coffee and making toast. We might have French toast on weekends. Sometimes when mom was tired Dad made eggs. Dad loved eggs. But Cocoa Puffs on a school morning was just fine. Stevie was squealing in wonder at how the milk at the bottom of the bowl had turned to chocolate milk. I had my own excitement to share, "Hey, I had a dream last night!"

"And what was that?" Mom said, matter-of-factly, expecting something cute perhaps. Maybe a superhero story. What do nine-year-olds dream about?

"Well, I was talking to God. And he was watching us. And you know what? He was laughing his butt off!"

"Young man, that's enough. That is using the Lord's name in vain! Now march right over there and write that on your sin chart! You must tell that sin to the priest during confession! Oh, my! I need to ask Father about the altar flowers before confession now. This will be so embarrassing!"

"But I can remember my dream! God was watching us like we were in a show. And He enjoyed it! People were doing crazy things and God laughed!"

"Enough of that or you will have a sin on your chart for disobeying! Goodness, you can't go around telling stories about talking to God! Do you understand? You just listen in church and that's all you need to know. Now, finish your Cocoa Puffs, the bus is coming."

Sister Meredith

Catechism. It wasn't fair. We had school all week and church on Sunday. We were supposed to be free on Saturday. Other kids got to go to Sunday school, and at least traded off church for catechism. No deal. We had catechism on Saturday morning for two hours.

The priest said it was that way so we wouldn't miss any part of the mass. Mom said it was that way to punish farm kids for not driving to town to attend the Catholic school. The Catholic school kids got religion during school, so they didn't need catechism.

I may have been the only kid to flunk catechism. I'm sure I don't remember the details, but somehow I ended up in my younger brother's class. Class was so long they gave us a fifteen-minute recess, and at least Stevie and I could hang out together. Mom and Grandma had arguments about my being "held back" while I suffered in the back seat riding to town for catechism on Saturday mornings. Couldn't sleep in, couldn't play, couldn't watch Saturday morning cartoons.

It seemed the catechism teachers were just as enthused about the whole arrangement until Sister Meredith arrived. She was too beautiful to be a nun, and yet there she was. She seemed to like us, too. "How are my young souls today!" she would waltz in singing. "You are souls given this life to do God's work."

"Wow," we thought, "this is different." We started paying attention to our souls. We were at a curious age, and Sister Meredith was happy to take our questions. The class peppered her with our curiosity. “Why do we die? What happens when my cow dies? What if someone eats my dead cow?”

“My dad says more people go to hell than heaven, is that true?”

“Will you go to hell for saying ‘damn’ because my dad says that all the time?”

The questions became exchanges around the classroom, “My dad says Father Bill is a priest because he likes to drink the communion wine.”

“That’s not wine, that’s blood!”

“Who do they get the blood from?”

“Cool, are priests vampires? Hey Sister, do priests bite you on the neck to make you nuns?”

“Do nuns wear habits to cover their neck bites? Is that why priests wear collars?”

The great mysteries were explored in catechism that year. Dad picked us up afterwards. “What did you learn today?” as we climbed into the pickup and squashed ourselves abreast of the dash.

“Priests have to bite girls on the neck to make them nuns.” Dad didn’t have any more questions. Mom and Grandma continued to have more discussions about my being held back.

Sister Meredith made catechism tolerable. One day the question came up, “Sister, why did God make us? What are we supposed to be for?” And Sister tried giving us the standard line we were God’s souls made to love Him and do His work. We were old enough, and bold enough, and pressed the soft-hearted Sister Meredith further. “God can do anything, He doesn’t need us to do His work. What are we really for?” We asked her how she knew what her soul was to do. Did we get to know when we turned 18? Is this the secret adults have about when people get married? Do we have a secret purpose in life? Why is it secret?

Sister Meredith stumbled on this, and we picked up on it. Kids can sense weakness yet haven't acquired the civility to hold back. "How did you know to become a nun? You're pretty, why didn't you get married and have kids? Do the old nuns pick on you like they do us kids?" She endured the personal onslaught until recess and brought us back to our studies afterward.

One blessed beautiful Saturday morning as we sat in a moldy church basement, the topic became more interesting. Sister Meredith described the crucifixion. There were nails, and spears, and blood. It seemed a good story, and Sister had our attention. She rhetorically asked, "What do you think it would be like to have nails pounded through your feet?" I raised my hand and offered to tell her. While reluctant to give up the momentum of her story telling, she cracked when I assured her I had all the "Jesus scars" and I could show them. The whole class saw this as an interesting continuation of the topic. Sister Meredith, trying her best to regain her momentum, revealed a moment of curiosity.

"Here, I'll start with my foot," and I whipped off a shoe and sock, revealing a nice inch long scar where a nail had pierced the top of my foot. The scar was just where medieval artist always placed the nails on the feet of the crucified Jesus.

"Look, he's had nails through his feet!" cried Jimmy, jumping out of his seat and doing the close-up inspection.

The scar had started as an idea and grew into a project. Stevie and I would set up a diving board at the end of the sand box. From this foot-and-a-half drop, we would dive into a blow up plastic pool. If you ever wonder what young boys do when locked out of the house on a summer day, this is it. Dad was working. Mom was off taking summer college classes. Carol, a high school age neighbor girl, would either let us watch TV or lock us out of the house so she and the girls could play in peace.

Stevie and I drug a big old board off the wood pile to form the diving platform. We hadn't removed the nails from it yet, but we planned to get to that at some point if the overall idea worked. We laid the board over the edge of the sand box and built a big sand pile to support and level the back end. We filled the pool and were ready to go.

I took a couple running steps toward the edge, expecting to bounce off the end, and splash down. Experience teaches far quicker than science class. As I reached the diving end of the board, with no counterweight at the other end, the board gave way and tipped. I tipped as well making a headlong dive into the pool. This would have been a minor setback, to be remedied by Stevie and I taking turns standing on the other end on the board. Perhaps we would have made revisions to roll a garbage barrel into place as a counterweight. But events progressed quickly. As my head went down, my feet went up, and as we all settled, the top side of my foot landed on a big old rusty nail.

I first noticed my nose hitting the bottom of the

plastic pool. I quickly became aware that breathing underwater was a problem. The messages from way down at my foot found their way to my brain in due time, and re-adjusted my focus. I pushed up and wiggled off the nail. Limping up the sidewalk, a scream and a bloody footprint were produced every other step. I climbed the porch and pounded on the door. Like normal, the girls ignored me, so it took considerable screaming and pounding to get results. Carol opened the door, “What did you do? You’re getting blood all over the porch! You’re not coming in here. Just wait while I get you a rag,” and she closed the door. I wrapped the rag on my foot and sat on the porch until mom came home. Stevie ran away for the rest of the day, thereby avoiding blame.

When mom got home, we made an immediate trip to the doctor. In those days, you saw a regular doctor at his office. If you were bleeding, they took you right past all the sick old people who could wait. Emergency rooms were for emergencies, so we never went there. “Hi, Doc.”

“Hello Gary, what are you in for today.” The doctor and I had gotten to know each other.

“There’s some blood coming out of my foot.” I explained.

“OK, let’s take a look. No reason to scream, the nurses would have to close the doors. You know, back in the war, I just cut a lot of these off. Too much bother to operate out there with a war going on all around. Out walking in the woods or something? Get stepped on by a cow? Oh well now, that’s quite a gash there, let’s see how deep that is. Jackie, why don’t you close the doors.”

I ended up with a tetanus shot, and my first "Jesus" scar.

Jimmy's fascination with the nail scar in my foot brought Sister Meredith over to inspect. Trying to regain control of the class she said, "Well Gary has suffered just a little bit of the pain Jesus endured. He has a scar to remind him how much forgiveness Jesus had to give him."

But it turned out I needed much more forgiveness. I had unbuttoned my shirt, prepared to show my next "Jesus scar". "How about this scar in my side?" as I opened half my shirt, revealing a two inch gash between a pair of ribs. Sister Meredith was taken aback. The boys crowded around for a closer view of the scar.

My uncle Denny was an electrician. As family stories are told, Denny was smart, because he had to study about electricity and take a test. It reasoned that he made "good money", and if we paid attention and studied at school, someday we could grow up to be electricians too. Noticing the complete lack of electricity in the fourth grade curriculum, I had to develop an independent understanding of electricity. Otherwise, I might be lost to farming all my life. A good place to start was the wall socket, and a bobby pin.

Electricity is an amazing thing, and I learned a great deal in a short time. I learned that electricity is stored up inside sockets as liquid blue hot stuff. If you tap it with a wire, it gushes out like striking an oil well, only with lightning. The shock wave blew my hand out of the way limiting the extent of the burns on my fingers. But the blue hot plasma ball jumped the distance to my rib cage and nicked me like a cowboy fighting Indians taking a flesh wound. It hurt like hell.

The doctor found this event far more interesting because they didn't have electrical injuries during the war. After trimming away the charred edges, he prescribed ointment and bandages.

"Hey, he got stabbed in the ribs by a spear!" exclaimed Jimmy.

"Yes, that's a remarkable scar, please everyone sit back down." Betraying her own instructions Sister Meredith leaned in closer for a look.

"And then there's these." Like a movie star in a hair cream ad, I smoothed back my bangs revealing a tire tread track of scars at the hair line.

There were big trees on the farm with great sweeping branches. Even some of the fruit trees were big enough to climb. As the fruit would ripen to a point just enough to get you sick, we would disappear amongst the leaves and eat like monkeys. We built tree houses and bird houses. And then, like every scar, it began with an idea.

Taken by the abilities of Tarzan to swing through the jungles the idea formed itself. Swinging on ropes seemed a far more efficient way to get from tree to tree compared to climbing down one to climb up another. Inspired, energetic, and locked out of the house, Stevie and I began our transformation of the orchard into the jungle. The walnut trees stood in a row at the edge of the orchard planted by an enterprising ancestor who knew that boys would need them to climb someday. They were the oldest and largest trees in the orchard, and the best place to put rope swings. The easiest place to start was from a treehouse we had erected, twenty feet up.

By doing the math in our heads, which meant taking a guess, Stevie and I climbed the neighboring walnut tree and shimmied out on a limb far enough to tie off the rope. We reached a height well above our tree house carrying coils of rope over our shoulders like Sherpas on the trail. I tied off the rope, and Stevie dropped the coils overboard. There was plenty of rope, so if things worked out, we could cut it off and make another "jungle vine". Everything was working out great. Perhaps for the last time, we climbed down the tree and then back up to the treehouse. Treetop transportation. It was time to test the system.

The plan was to swing from the treehouse over to a branch on the next tree at about the same height. We tied the rope to a point on a branch well overhead that extended part way across the gap. This project was thought out in detail, and we were considering the improvements and options for the next tree. I wrapped the rope around my fore-arm for extra gripping power, pulled hard to check the knot, and then stepped over the edge.

Almost everything went according to plan. The knot held, the rope held, the swing of the arc to the other tree was clear of obstructions. However, we failed to consider how adding an extra sixty pounds to the branch would lower this reference point. Thus, the branch sagged, and I came sweeping in with the speed of a bird without the benefit of wings two feet below the target. I tried pulling my feet up to land them, but cognition and reaction were too late. A precision impact at face level occurred. Some great teacher in the sky had planned the event for maximum educational value, driving lessons directly into my skull. By some miracle I hung on to the rope. Stunned and spinning I failed to align for a landing approach on the return flight to the treehouse. Still swinging two feet below the original launch pad, I came in at face height right to the platform. Another precision collision right to the forehead.

Wrapping the rope around one's forearm is an effective method to keep your grip. Despite two collisions I went right on swinging. Having scraped up the treehouse, I went for a return whack at the other tree. As the science experiment continued to reveal its lessons, I discovered that a rope fastened at a single point is not limited to one plane of operation. I was now swinging in something of a circle at the bottom of a cone tipping about its point. Several great misses occurred at each end of the swing until I reached out with a leg and harnessed a small lower branch against the trunk of the far tree. There I hung for a moment, a leg over a branch, an arm tangled up in the rope. I wiggled the rope free and tumbled down the side of the tree. Stevie came running up to have a look at me. After sizing up the situation he disappeared for the rest of the day.

"Oh man, that's like scars from a crown of thorns!" Jimmy and a few of the other kids were ecstatic that Sister Meredith's tales of execution had produced a real-life survivor. "How did you get those scars? Man, who tried to crucify you? Are those real?"

Sister Meredith seemed to have lost the moment, caught up in her own thoughts and staring at my forehead. After a contemplative look she turned and went to the front of the class. "Ok class, now we move on to Easter. Has anyone risen from the dead before?"

The look in my direction suggested I not raise my hand.

The next year, Stevie and I advanced to the next level of catechism. Sister Meredith was gone. We heard she had married and was expecting a baby. I guess sometimes your purpose in life changes.

Purpose

"Enjoying a sound night's rest?"

"Oh yes, God. There's a gentle spring rain on the roof, and distant thunder. Just the right mix to let me sleep and slip away. I love being here on the edge of heaven. It is refreshing."

"Shall we do some work while you are resting?"

"OK. You lead, of course."

"Look there at a young man in the seminary. I have not called him to be a priest, but he and his family believe it is his destiny. Can you feel his loneliness? Can you see he is lost? He will need to stand up to strong-willed parents one day. But I am leading him there. Learn to follow My lead. If you listen just a little, you will make your way to your purpose. Don't be afraid or resist because it is Me tugging at you."

"Let's look at someone who knows how to follow you."

"There we go. Do you see that man pulling on a rope to tie off a ship at a dock? He seems plain. Yet he goes about his work with joy. He loves people as he meets them. And every morning he opens his eyes, thanks me, and asks me to guide his hands. He has many good days and few worries. When times are difficult for him he finds Me. Now, look over there..."

Dreams

School would let out and we ran to the bus. After a short dusty ride we ran from the bus at our stop. It seemed natural. I'm not sure what the hurry was. Perhaps we sensed so little day was left for opportunities to play. Perhaps there was some irresistible freedom we burst upon jumping down from the last step. Whatever it was, we ran. To the barn, to the pasture, to the orchard, we just ran.

Upon achieving our objective of the orchard one afternoon, Stevie and I climbed to our favorite perches in the apple tree and commenced ruining our dinner. We looked up through the tree leaves at a perfect blue sky shining back. I nestled into an odd crook on an old branch, formed from a healed over break from years before. Chomping away on an apple I ventured, "Hey, I had a dream last night."

"What was it?" Stevie, was always interested in the telling of a great tale.

"I was sitting on a hill talking to God. And he showed me these neat people and the stuff they had done. They were just regular folks that nobody knows. We'd be talking, and then He would swoosh his arm across the sky and we could watch another person like a giant movie. But it was better than that. I was right there with them. I could feel stuff and smell stuff and could even tell what they were thinking."

"That sounds awesome. Did you see any pirates?"

"No, but I saw a doctor operate on a dog."

"Cool. I wish I had dreams."

"You do. You have to sort of wake up during them."

"Any more?"

"I saw a guy working on an airplane. Another mowing hay, and a lady holding a baby. I saw a bunch of people at a Christmas party. I saw more working on big hot pipes in the ground, and a man with a long grey beard and dirty clothes with a cat. God liked these people. He said they were special gifts for me. It sounds kinda boring, but I guess you had to be there. I think everyone I saw was doing something God liked."

"God likes cats?"

"It was weird, but I could feel that the cat was really old but felt good sitting on the old man. I think God was telling me I could do lots of things and he would be happy. Those folks are doing things God enjoys."

"Would God like us sitting in trees eating apples?"

"Yup, it seems right."

Janice

There are people you grow up with called aunts and uncles and cousins. After a while you figure out these people used to be your parent's family when they were kids. Sometimes, these people turn back into kids when they are together, but that's just the way aunts, uncles, and cousins are. Even mom and dad acted odd. You never know about relatives.

Out of this bushel basket of odd-balls, a few were just like family. The best of these was aunt Janice. Janice was mom's younger sister. Mom came from a farm family with fifteen kids, so to be "older" or "younger" never provided much information. But she seemed a lot younger than mom and we liked her.

There are fond memories bouncing on a bed with Suzy, Stevie, and Janice, who must have been a teenager. While Janice was babysitting we bobbed up and down between bare light bulbs hanging by cords from the ceiling. Dad was filling his free time remodeling the attic into our bedrooms. Between working a job and farming it was taking a while, and our future bedrooms were just fine as a playroom. We had new floppy furry slippers we could show off as we bounccd up high and lifted our feet.

Janice was fun and happy and could turn grass and wind and sunshine into a great day. But she was afraid of creatures dead or alive. We had to run through the pasture to keep grasshoppers from landing on us. We had to keep our distance from the cows. The chickens were manic pecking monsters. Stevie and I collected eggs every day, but Janice ran from the chickens. Barns and basements were off limits and even damp shady places gave her the creeps. But her fear of critters made her an excellent story teller. We piled into bed with popcorn and Dr. Pepper. There she told great scary stories that were all true about snakes crawling up pant legs, wild cattle trampling villages into dust, and flies breeding in refrigerators on old food. For some reason she kept saying she was glad to move off grandpa's farm.

For a while, Janice lived with us. She was going to nursing school, and we lived near the edge of town. Grandpa and Grandma still farmed somewhere way out in the wild country, making us the most convenient relatives to impose upon. Pressed into service to watch us kids, a deal was done and Janice was family.

Mom and dad, always afraid of starving to death, were entrepreneurs of a sort. There was always another way, involving hard work and less sleep, to avoid starving to death. Dad worked for Texaco and managed to raise calves, chickens, hay, and tended an orchard. Mom taught school, raised a market garden and sold stainless steel cookware to anyone polite enough to listen. One day a man wearing a soft plaid businessman's hat showed up and talked to dad in the driveway for a while. Friends and family were invited in the house. Business meetings occurred outside. At dinner that night, dad started talking about chinchillas.

It turned out chinchillas were in great demand. The world could not find enough of these little creatures. Like small rabbits, with thicker softer fur, their hides were bringing top prices. If an enterprising fellow could set up cages, water and feed them a bit of alfalfa, they would spontaneously reproduce into an explosion of dollar bills.

As the discussion went on at the table, we kids listened. Another great experiment was hatching. But a problem developed. The barn was already full of cows and chickens. While a shed could be built, it was winter and the chinchilla market was booming right now! The garage was off limits as mom was not going to start scraping snow off the windows with the car parked outside. The debate played like ping pong across the dinner table until settling on a temporary arrangement. A couple of breeding pairs would be set up for the initial explosive breeding period in the back room of the basement. When spring came a shed would be built and the business could expand.

The basement was another family playground. We road tricycles and shot dart guns in the basement. We played on an old piano. Dad had spare bits of lumber and a Folger's coffee can of recovered nails. He encouraged us to practice our hammering skills. There were big plans for us some day involving tools. We might nail four old thread spools to a board and exclaim, "Hey, look at the car I built!"

"That's really good son. Pretty soon you can start using fence pliers."

In the basement, there was a functioning root cellar behind one wall. Full of canned vegetables and fruit, a sand bed in the floor held carrots and parsnips. Onions were strung over wires, and fresh apples sat in bushel baskets behind another door. As further protection against starving to death, I guess the fruit cellar was necessary. Perhaps it was kept full in case the relatives showed up starving to death one day. Hard times were haunting.

But space for chinchillas was needed. The back room was cleared, the piano moved to one side. Cages were built four high along three walls. An open topped cage ran down the center of the room. Watering and food trays were wired to the cages because the little chinchillas would spill them if left loose. The whole set was raised off the floor. Plastic, paper, and sawdust was positioned under the cages. Construction was exciting and built our anticipation of rearing chinchillas.

We didn't get a couple pair of breeding chinchillas. To our delight and mom's surprise, twelve breeding pairs and sixty little ones arrived. Soft grey balls of fur, they looked like ground squirrels with wispy tails and rabbit ears. With food and water waiting, they were introduced to their cages, and we giggled with delight. Around the cages they ran and tumbled into one another. The chinchillas weren't mean, but they were willing to bite anything they could touch. Cute little squeaks and barks filled the basement as they told each other of their new homes.

By the next morning, the fun became chores. Feed, water, and new papers. Even children were capable of these simple chores. The responsibility of feeding or starving the chinchillas to death was laid upon our delicate young minds. Compared to some chores, it was not bad. The chinchillas were glad to see us and devoured their food and water the instant we filled their cups. I expect their instincts suggested they were going to starve to death, so they were right at home. They grew as fast as chia pets with beautiful soft coats.

Dad had certain chores with the chinchillas as well. One morning we found him hard at work performing little dental adjustments to the chinchillas. It turned out they had sharp teeth that needed to be regularly put to use or they would grow. Like little beavers, they needed things to gnaw and chew. Our discovery occurred when chinchillas began to show up in unusual places around the house. One evening, a shadow bolted along the wall behind the couch. Mom screamed, "It's a mouse!"

Suzy screamed, "I saw it. It was a giant mouse. It was a rat! And it had a furry tail!"

Dad figured it out, cornered the little critter and sent him back with his friends. He discovered the chinchillas were chewing holes in the cages. Thereafter, we deposited blocks of wood, old pots and pans, toys, whatever it seemed they might gnaw. They were happy to chew most things, and it slowed the cage chewing somewhat. As time passed, a loose chinchilla event was more mundane. The shadowy flash across the room would appear, "hey kids, stop wrestling and get that chinchilla back to the basement." Mom would gaze over her coffee cup watching Bonanza without spilling a drop.

Janice had moved in without knowing we had a budding chinchilla business in the basement about to explode into millions of dollars. With several entrepreneurial ventures underway at all times, it skipped our minds to inform her. Janice settled in to the living room to sleep on the couch while dad accelerated efforts to complete the new bedrooms in the attic. The next morning, Janice seemed upset. She said she had seen an animal roaming around the living room. Stevie and I went exploring, and all we could find was a pair of furry floppy slippers. All was well, except for a bit of shy embarrassment.

The next morning Janice was upset again. “Last night the wind settled down, and the house stopped shaking and creaking. Did you notice that?” Of course we always noticed when the house stopped shaking and creaking in the wind. During those quiet still winter nights the noises from town traveled great distances. Train whistles, factory sounds, big trucks shifting gears. “Well,” she continued, “I heard noises coming from the basement. Hacking raspy sounds, grating noises, shuffling sounds, and squeals. Something is living under the house.” Stevie and I rushed away from our Cocoa Puffs to the basement to look for what possible monsters were keeping Janice awake. We reported back, having found no treacherous creatures. We even looked in the root cellar.

Something happened that next night. We aren’t sure what it was. Janice woke up the whole house screaming and running. At one point, she ran into the cold winter night refusing to come back in the house. Janice moved to the unfinished attic the next day. Dad started building a new shed in the dead of winter. It was an odd thing to do. But you never know what might happen when the relatives show up.

Every Blessed Day

"How's my little soul? Taking a rest from your great journey?"

"Dear God, I am perplexed. It seems every blessed day is pointless. I am losing focus on my real purpose and getting nowhere! Nothing but distractions. I don't see how my adventure can lead to where you intended me to go."

"Patience little soul. Why don't you tell me about your day?"

"It seems a wasted day. This childhood is blissful but aimless. I'm quite grateful, but anxious as well. Today, is a good example.

"Today was a school day, so breakfast was cereal and milk and toast. Mom made instant mix cocoa and Stevie and I dipped our toast in it. The morning was bright and brisk, so we watched for the school bus from inside the porch, and ran out to it as it pulled up. The bus ride bounced us along roads through busy farms with wispy smoke coming off chimneys, and animals venturing out from barns. The Simpson chicken farm really stunk when we pulled up to it this morning, so we teased Kyle and Jeff when they got on the bus.

"School, predictable and typical. Reading out loud in our reading circle, a timed math test, a recess, story time. At recess we kicked balls to see whose could go the farthest.

"After school, we must find our cousins and walk them home because they're too little. We stay at Aunt Janice's house until mom comes by and picks us up. I

guess we skip the long bus ride home that way. Aunt Janice was fun today. They have a big two story square house with porches on two sides. She was on the porch swing, and we all took turns riding it. She had the windows open and music playing, and after a while she started teaching us how to dance out on the porch. Mom came and talked to Janice and had coffee. We went back to swinging.

"When we got home we watched TV, and mom made dried beef over toast for supper. Dad enjoyed it and told us an army story. Stevie and I got our little plastic soldiers out and played until Red Skelton came on. After that, off to bed, into our dreams, and here I am."

"Sounds like a good day."

"Yes, I have many good days. Lots of little pleasures, thank You! But they are unproductive. I'm just marking off time."

"I am with you every day, so I'll tell you more about today. Things you may not notice. First, Kyle and Jeff were very embarrassed on the bus this morning. They and their mother are working hard to take care of their chicken farm while their dad recovers from an accident. He lost an arm in a corn sheller two weeks ago, and while he'll be fine, this little family is doing their best to overcome a challenge. You added to their challenge this morning.

"Did you notice everyone reading in your circle this morning? Miss Ripker is very proud of her class because every one of you are reading with confidence. She had a good day that you were part of.

"You are on a great adventure with a purpose, but you are also part of many other adventures. Today

was just a normal day for you, and you played a part in Kyle's day, and Miss Ripker's day. There was another purpose today that you helped Me with.

"You took your cousins home, and there was Janice, swinging on the porch swing and crying. Did you notice she was crying? No? And her girls went right to the swing, but you stopped and gave her a big hug. Do you remember that? No? And yes, you were the big boy, so while the kids were swinging, she taught you how to dance. A little thing.

"Last night, your uncle came home drunk and beat her. You didn't notice the makeup covering her black eyes. Janice must raise three strong willed independent girls. They have important things to do one day. To accomplish this, Janice will endure much. Today, she was thinking of suicide, so I sent her a little love and you delivered it. She'll be fine for a while, and will find a way to get her girls on their path.

"After that, I will give Janice a kindness. She will have a brain tumor, and without notice I will call her home. Her adventure will be shorter than most. With the work she is doing, she deserves an early trip home. It will also send her girls off to greater things, a push they will need. I'll let you remember this little dream the day Janice comes back to Me. You will feel injustice and pain on that day. But knowing this, you will feel a sweetness to help you along.

"Even while you are young you will visit the lonely, encourage friends, and spark hope and ambition. Your impact upon others will grow as you do. Work on your purpose will become more deliberate. Now back you go, for another normal day."

Jane

Love was something new. I didn't expect it. Girls were a thing I paid little attention to. They tended to get boys in trouble. Best avoided.

Love started at recess. Those delightful breaks we could be free for twenty minutes to pursue battles. We had a hill, a ledge, a dirt lot, and a paved lot. The dirt lot supported grass when school was out, and sprouted swings and slides and teeter totters. There was a crazy machine you could grab a handle, lift your feet, and swing around in circles at the end of a chain. With lots of riders we were supposed to all go around the same direction, and mostly we didn't. We made mountains from snow. We made roads in the dirt. We made trouble when there was mud. We always came in dirtier, happier, and disappointed it was over. It was war and peace and soon, I discovered, it was love.

On that day, we were playing marbles. Our version of marbles had two players dump their marbles on the dirt, inscribed by a circle drawn by a finger. With our shooters we took turns knocking marbles out of the circle. The teachers told us we couldn't play for keeps, as if that would have been fun. My opponent was getting the best of me, having cleaned me out of half my marble stock.

Amidst the contented and happy clamor of a recess, a commotion arose. The industrial arts building at the edge of the playground ejected a tall skinny kid. It was Stuart. He was on our bus route and lived in a junkyard in a valley back in the hills.

This was one of the high school kids you ran away from, and never ever sat in front of on the school bus. Right behind him came his brother John. John was a grizzly bear wearing a letter jacket. While John could crush beer cans on his head, we weren't afraid of him because he made a regular practice of rescuing little kids from Stuart. But Stuart had him mad this time.

A percussive smack cut through the peaceful banter of the playground. A symphony of sounds erupted. The soprano screams of the girls. The alto shouts from the recess teacher. Stuart and John added barking low tones in harmony. A crescendo of quick, violent, and rising notes. John caught Stuart mid-playground, grabbed his shirt and flung him on the ground as if trying to kill a snake. Stuart rolled and spit and hissed like a mad rattler.

The student body ringed the combatants leaving room for adjustments in the action. Even at that, the fight broke through the circle at one point, the line weaving, re-forming, and re-adjusting to the new lines of battle. Irresistible fear held the line, no one leaving, everyone glued to attention.

We knew this was a good one when the teacher went running to the building, allowing the battle to reach its natural level of intensity without interruption. We were excited that John might finally kill Stuart, and that would make bus rides much easier. But Stuart landed some good licks on John, too. You could hear the smack when a solid punch hit. But John was prevailing, his superior mass absorbing the blows better, and throwing Stuart to the dirt with regularity. The end-of-recess bell rang. We ignored it. Not even the girls left the circle. Mr. Burns showed up just as the blood flowed. He had immense power of presence as this five-and-a-half-foot middle-aged war veteran stepped between the brothers, grabbed each by a collar, and marched them to the school. He said nothing. The fight was over.

The teacher re-appeared and blew her whistle signaling us to line up. Then, I noticed Jane was standing at my side just behind me grabbing my arm. I looked at her and fell in love. She ran off to get in line. That was it, love introduced itself.

We were in fourth grade, and our teacher was Mrs. Bogan. She read to us after recess as we listened and "wound down" after recess. During this time, she dismissed us one by one to use the bathroom. For some reason she didn't trust us to use the bathrooms in groups. There were two timers on her desk, one for the boys, one for the girls. Mrs. Bogan would give a nod and start your timer for your bathroom break. It was a well-practiced routine, and she could manage the timers and dismissals without skipping a word.

A few days passed since the fight, and while listening to Mrs. Bogan read she nodded toward me for my turn. I hurried because we were at a good point in the story. Our classroom was in the second floor of the school building. Years before a new section of the school was built. The new and improved building lined up level on the first floor, but the second floor ended up three feet higher than the old building's second floor. Thus, a descending ramp had been constructed in the hallway connecting the two parts of the building. The full width of the hallway, a three-foot drop over a twenty-foot length. A nice shiny ramp with white vinyl tiles, waxed to a shine and slippery as a ski slope. In the winter as we lined the halls taking our boots off, we ended up in our socks. Socks, ramp, wax, an architectural funhouse. What boy between six and forty could hold themselves back? The ramp was fun whenever it wasn't patrolled. Real trouble occurred the day we lined ourselves up like bowling pins, and Christopher ran down the hall and rolled like a ball into the pile. But innocent accidental sliding was bound to happen.

My bathroom break was short as I was in a hurry to get back to the story. As I came out of the bathroom and headed for the ramp, I saw Jane coming from the other direction. Our eyes met just as she reached the top of the ramp. She stared for a moment. I could tell something deep was happening. I stopped at the bottom of the ramp and stared into her eyes across the rise. A strange "butterflies-in-the-stomach" feeling swelled within me. Somewhere music played, landscapes appeared, sweet smells wafted, and time stopped. And then she threw up. A great big circle of semi-processed lunch hit near the top of the ramp at her feet. The more liquid parts made thick little streams like syrup on pancakes, running down the white tiled ramp.

Jane had broken our loving gaze and now seemed embarrassed. She covered her mouth with her hands, tip-toed around the mess, and ran for the girl's bathroom. I likewise tip-toed around the trickling soupy scene and made my way back to the classroom. Taking my seat, Mrs. Bogan swatted the timer and nodded to Clark, the next kid behind me, for his turn. The story continued, but somehow I wasn't listening. Jane must have felt some of that "butterflies-in-the-stomach" feeling just like I did, but she couldn't handle it and threw up. And that meant we were in love! The sun pouring through the windows was softer. Time passed slower. Mrs. Bogan's voice was a distant radio. While contemplating the depth of our relationship, Clark came bursting back, "some kid threw up on the ramp! It's totally gross!"

Mrs. Bogan gave us the "be good or I'll kill you look" and skirted out to the hallway. After a while Clark came back. "It was Jane. She's going to the office!" The class went on asking Clark for detailed descriptions of the mess. Jane was a good kid. Good kids don't go to the office. I worried about her seeing Mr. Burns. That's what love does. You worry about others. I wasn't sure if they spanked kids who threw up on the floor. I knew they spanked you if you broke things, like windows or chairs or if six kids climbed up on a hand rail and accidentally broke it. It seemed wrong if Jane was getting spanked because she fell in love with me and unfortunately threw up. There was nothing to be done. A new feeling. Helplessness to act on behalf of someone I loved! For something I caused! Love was agony.

Spring arrived. Jane and I got up the courage to talk to one another. We would shift spots at lunch to sit across the table. We found chairs in music class side by side. We walked together out the school door to say, "See you tomorrow!" But summer came. With summer came freedom, and long days to roam our bit of country side. But other than fireworks on the fourth of July, and the county fair, we didn't see most of our classmates. That meant a long summer without Jane. I had never missed my friends before, preferring freedom to moments of fun with the boys on the playground. Love brought complications. Love brought longing and loneliness.

At the supper table one evening mom had news for dad, “Did you see in the paper! Jack died! He was driving a night run and fell asleep at the wheel. He ran off the road into an embankment. They found him dead. Look, there’s a picture in the newspaper. What a shame, four kids. Whatever will Maggie do? I know he was taking those extra jobs after farming all day, but it’s just not worth it. Kids, don’t one of you have one of their kids in class? Isn’t Jane in your class?” And it was true. Jane had lost her father in a tragic accident. People had died before. Relatives, neighbors. I had not met Jane’s dad, but felt a tremendous sorrow. Another complication that came with love. I spent the next few weeks worrying about Jane, wondering what I would say, and wanting to make her feel better.

School came. We found our new room assignments and settled in. I didn’t see Jane and figured she was assigned to another homeroom class. Darn, it would be a long year. With three home rooms per grade level, we sorted each other out at recess, but I couldn’t find Jane. The next day I found some of Jane’s friends and asked where she was. “Oh, Jane’s dad died. So, her mom moved them away to live with her aunt for a while.” It was the only explanation I ever got. I could never help her nor see her again. Love hurts.

Love and War

I learned two things in sixth grade. I learned about love and war. The rest of sixth grade didn't matter. A problem with our brains is that we don't remember normal stuff. We remember the out-of-the-ordinary things. And for sixth grade, things were pretty normal.

Then there were the odd details forever stuck in memory. My favorite baseball bat used at recess. A thirty-four inch Wilson that I could connect to a pitch. How the melting and freezing runoff from a neighboring farm built up in the schoolyard to make awesome brown and yellow shades in the ice we slid on. The macaroni and cheese at the school cafeteria. The blockhouse addition to the bus barn used as a music room. Pointless but vivid memories.

The events leading up to the fight were indistinct. I know my friends and I were darned sick and tired of Dean. Dean was the class bully. He had a natural inclination to make people mad and took great delight in it. From the school bus, to gym class, to lunch period, and the marches between, he never missed opportunities to create trouble. Recess was his free reign to bully time, and he was always interrupting someone's good fun. Getting hauled off to the principal's office by the recess teacher with regularity never reformed his manner.

The fight happened one winter day at recess. The school was propped on a hill providing natural slopes for sliding. Rules were enforced that we couldn't bring sleds or equipment to school after too many pile ups had resulted in ripped clothes and broken bones. Equipment being banned, we slid on our backs and our bellies. The natural progression of unintended consequences followed the new rules. If you had good leather shoes, and good balance, you could ski on your feet. Slick coats became popular. But without professional equipment, our sliding courses had to be groomed. After a good snow, we organized ourselves to spend a whole recess getting a solid track stomped into icy firmness. Then we would slide, pulling each other like grading equipment. Lying on backs and bellies we pushed ourselves, smoothing out the hard lumpy packed snow. The final step involved filling and polishing rough spots by hand into a virtual bobsled run. After a hard recess or two, days and days of high speed sliding followed.

The teachers never minded we were destroying our clothing, getting soaking wet and catching pneumonia. We were busy and happy and not causing trouble, so the recess teacher could spend her time talking to girls and hauling Dean off to the principal.

We had been enjoying a wet bloodless recess when Dean came over and carved a big cross wise groove in our polished glass track. It was the final straw. A short meeting of the guys convened, and a decision reached. Now was the time to pound the snot out of Dean. I volunteered to provoke the first blow. Turning out from the group, I called Dean a name, and challenged him to come over for a pounding.

Always enjoying a good fight, Dean complied, stomping up our track, with his mouth in high gear. The plan was simple, I would pound him, and if Dean started getting the best of me, everyone else would join in. I swung and landed the first blow. Shocked at the challenge, Dean swung and missed. I swung again, and while I landed a fist on his chest, he grabbed my arm. At this point, we twisted, slipped and fell.

Landing on the bottom is an unfortunate position if you are trying to pound the snot out of a bully. The rest of the crew, looking for any sign I was in trouble, piled on. A mob of boys swinging and hollering and rolling in the snow. It was a giant fighting snowball. On my back I was still able to get in several satisfying punches. Effective or not, they felt good.

Somehow old Mrs. Leach, the recess teacher, made it down our track without falling, and peeled the snowball apart. She had witnessed everything, standing a dozen feet away when I landed the first punch. Confused about marching me off the playground, instead of Dean, she didn't take me to the principal's office right away. We stopped by the corner of the school where she interrogated me about what was wrong. With her back to the playground, my allies saw their opportunity, and pounded some more snot out of Dean. I was not answering the questions well, somewhat distracted and bemused by the brawl going on fifty feet behind Mrs. Leach. She was hard of hearing, but eventually my rapt attention caught her attention, and she turned to see playground pandemonium. It seemed every kid who had ever been picked on by Dean was joining the fight and getting in a couple licks. They had him bleeding and crying and rolling on the ground. It was a great recess to remember.

Mrs. Leach left me and ran for the new pile,

becoming a strange ally with the class bully. Protecting him from everyone else the familiar march off the playground began, but this time heading for the school nurse.

The bell rang, and we lined up as if nothing special had happened. Mrs. Leach marched by arm wrapped in armpit with Dean and told us to let ourselves in as she hurried by. We stood around in line wondering what exactly that meant. After a time, some girl started acting like the teacher and organized us well enough to march ourselves back to class.

Dean continued to be a bully that year, but never bothered me again. This was the day I learned the most in sixth grade. If you are provoked into a fight, surprise your enemy, bring friends, and don't stop until you are done.

The second thing we learned in sixth grade was about love. My friend Jerry, had written a love note. It was silly and gooey. All it needed were names for the suitor and the pursued. With reciprocating notes, we could manipulate two unexpected love birds into a romance. We chose with deliberation and care. Both recipients had to be under the twenty-fifth percentile in the class. We figured this was maximizing the believability of the love letters and minimizing the chance they would ever figure out we were writing the notes.

Our downfall was our enjoyment, and hence our zeal to make each letter more extreme. While tame by modern standards, the "wishes for kisses" and "hot to hold hands" message got through. After several days of letter exchanges, the erstwhile pair were manipulated into a recess meeting by the corner of the school past the swings. The real live meeting did not go well for us. While we might have held slim hopes for a playground hug, instead the ruse was exposed. It was a turn of events we had never considered. But we had a great time watching from across the playground.

Something gave us away. The pile of boys rolling on the ground and laughing our butts off might have been a clue. But the break up almost became disaster. Somehow old Mrs. Leach was informed. During class after recess when Mrs. Leach would normally read great literature to us, she decided to have a serious conversation with the class. After the lecture about hurt feelings and embarrassment, she shocked us all and read the last letter out loud. This was her effort to shame the culprits into exposing themselves and saying they were sorry.

It hurt. It really hurt. I never felt so bad in my life. Containing great waves of belly busting laughter, without cracking a smile can be a most painful exercise. I held my side. I held my mouth. I had to look under my desk to exhale and breath. But I got through it. And that was the second thing I learned in sixth grade. Love can hurt, but it's almost always worth it.

Free Will

"I find you alone at the edge? Something is bothering My little soul."

"Must we hurt each other all day? Kids and adults alike get angry and fight. A day, a year, a decade later it becomes silly, but we flare up in near moments. We find creative ways to hurt each other. Even when we make friends or love each other, we take occasion to hurt. Sometimes we are hurt by events, not of our own making. Why did you make us this way? Is it not Your way? Yet there we are."

"Yes, the conditions I set up allow for conflict and bad behavior. It allows for tragedy and pain. We've discussed how effort and yes, pain bring qualities to love and joy. There is another dimension to this. Much of your pain you have chosen. It is your free will, or that of others as you allow."

"How can my pain be something I chose?"

"How you choose is your free will. How you respond along your journey will determine much of your path. I'm sure by now you have heard the golden rule, 'Do unto others as you would have done unto yourself.' My boy Luke was very succinct with that one, and Matthew dressed it up a bit. That's a good start. As you grow, you are finding people that are taking advantage of power or position. You have no ability to change their behavior. Leave them be. My Son had another answer, didn't He? Turn the other cheek? Shake the dust from your sandals? When asked the greatest commandment, what did He say? 'Love God and love your neighbor as you love yourself.' Just a reminder, when he was

coming home to me he said, 'Love one another as I have loved you.' These become your actual choices, and your exercise of free will.

"You notice there was no condition in there, such as, 'If you love me, I'll love you. If you are kind, I'll be kind.' People struggled with My Son's message. They looked for power and advantage. They tried to cover their insecurities, shame, and failings. Many wouldn't risk extending goodness first, without expectation of returns. There was immense power available in His message and His actions, but they could not see. In the end, they crucified Him."

"What will happen if I treat people badly?"

"As I said, your choices will set much of your path. The lessons and experiences you encounter will be your result. Much is learned while recovering from such a journey. Or it can be an unfortunate squandering of a grand adventure. There are souls who set out on difficult paths. But poor is not bad. Destitute is not lost from Me. Enslaved, imprisoned, abused does not require a desperate response. Take your situation and follow the good. Greet with joy. Start and end your days with Me.

"Some are well cared for yet unfulfilled. The bits of dust you are and live with are not your objective. They leave you hungry. Little soul, pause your waking mind to think and wonder. It is the Spirit, not the dust you seek.

"Listen to the regrets of the dying. They wish for more of the people and experiences they enjoyed. Seek joy. Look for it in people, in work, in accomplishment, in service and you will find it. Follow it. Bring to Me your joyful struggle. We will have a fine time reviewing your

journey when you come home.”

“For those who are evil, what of them?”

“That’s always up to Me. These are souls of My making. There have been many warnings given. My Son repeated such warnings. Do you want to review such a life as you come to join Me? To bring such a gift to my door causes souls great anguish. Concern yourself with your own journey.”

“And then, what of the pain, loneliness, and setbacks?”

“Can you love someone before they love you? Can you spend your day working without complaint? Can you visit the lonely and assist your neighbor? Do you know your gifts and use them? And if struggles appear while you serve others, can you be strong like a sapling to bend in the wind, allow the storms to pass, and resume becoming a great creature? Were these not messages My Son taught? What pain would you encounter if you began every day with such a mission?

“You’re about to wake up with great confusing thoughts. Let’s see how you do!”

Hills

Dad and Grandpa were sitting on the cistern. A flat wood top built up over our underground water supply. Stevie and I were playing in the sandbox. As dusk fell, the breeze dropped off, and locusts revved up their melancholy buzz, foreshadowing the end of summer. A quiet late summer evening is a piece of heaven. I could hear Dad and Grandpa engrossed in one of their deep conversations. They were wondering about the purpose of the hills.

"Look," Dad said, "God put the earth here, made the wind blow and water fall, and here we have these hills. They must have some purpose. We haven't figured it out yet." Grandpa talked about lifting us higher to see a farther horizon. He was old enough to be philosophical.

I walked up and squeezed between them and listened for a while. As a kid, the answer was obvious. Hills are made to go down.

Sunny windy summer days allowed a kid opportunity to get out of vocal range. If we got past the barn, no one could bother us, because we couldn't hear their hollering, anyway. And so today's adventure began in the barn. Dad seemed to have a source for paper barrels. They were sturdy barrels of dense cardboard with metal rings holding both ends, and a thick solid cardboard bottom. We didn't know what they were built for, but sometimes dad would come home with a couple more paper barrels. He would sort his junk into these barrels for storage. Bits of wood, steel fence posts in another, chicken feed, wire, all sorted by category into paper barrels in the barn. But today we found an empty one. Dad must have run out of time to re-organize his stash into more refined categories. We seized the moment.

The barrel went outside, and we followed it. We tried log rolling on it. If you're going to fall down, you might as well climb a tree. We crawled inside and rolled around, which was much more fun. The problem was, it wasn't a self-sustaining action. Someone had to keep pushing the barrel. The natural course to follow would be the hill.

We lived atop a ridge of hills with gradual rolling tops in most directions, but steep sides to the east. The steeper sections were left to pasture and the grass could be found of various heights for hay or grazing. Many routes had been discovered for tobogganing. We knew the longest, the fastest, the one with the jumps, the one with the mean curves. In the summer we would attempt the routes with our bicycles. The spokes would tear the heads off the grass and throw them in every direction. Our jeans and shoes would be grass stained and our arms covered in little cuts and scratches. Riding down a steep pasture hill on a bicycle was terrifying and painful and ended in crashes. It was irresistible.

It was with this high hope for expanding the adventures of the hill that we rolled out the barrel. Figuring we didn't know how to steer yet, we picked a route farthest from the fences. With our concern for fences, we overlooked a detail that this route had a little bonus ski jump two thirds of the way down the slope. Foxes had dug a den into the hillside and left a depression. The tailings from the digging formed an immediate hump downhill from the depression. Riding a toboggan over this jump became a test to see if you could stay upright upon landing. You had to lay long and low and hang on to the toboggan. If you let go the rider and toboggan had different flight dynamics, and would plunge into separate snow banks. Often, the toboggan found its way to a long walk down the valley. It was best to hang on regardless of the outcome.

Stevie and I crawled into the barrel and began our roll. The hill was quite effective at providing the self-sustaining rolling action we were seeking. We had overlooked another detail. With two boys laying lengthwise in a barrel that is rolling, this is what happens on the inside, “I squash you, you squash me, I squash you, you squash me… repeat thirty thousand times.” We were two logs in a barrel. Our guardian angels laughed for a while before taking pity, veering us sideways and spilling us out. We crawled around, laid on the pasture, and watched the clouds swirl around in a blue sky. The clouds are beautiful when they swirl like that.

Experience is just learning things the hard way, so we rolled the paper barrel up the hill and applied our fresh experience. It was determined we would crawl into the barrel and assume fetal positions, stacked side by side like refrigerated dough for dinner rolls in a tube. This would prevent the squashing problem, and might enhance the rolling sensation. Again, the hill provided more than adequate self-sustaining action for rolling the barrel. We discovered another curiosity about how the universe works. When you put two boys in a barrel and roll them, they always end up parallel to the axis of the rolling apparatus and squashing each other. Just two logs in a barrel. With the same result and a few more bruises, we had to change the approach.

A plan was made to take turns. This would eliminate the squashing problem. I conceded my elder pecking order position with mature decorum. I could study Stevie's ride with a clear head, and record his death if things went wrong. Off he went. From the top of the hill, I could see the barrel gathering speed, running in a nice straight line, and then... wow that lift off the fox den was unexpected. It looked like the barrel even kept spinning while it was in the air.

After I heard the landing, and watched it come to rest some two-hundred yards away, I decided I would walk down to help push the barrel back up for my turn. I found the barrel first. It rolled all the way to the fence at the bottom of the hill. We never made it to the fence while tobogganing because the snow would drift in deep and we would burrow in like snow plows, buried up to our chins. But the barrel lacked a braking system, so it made sense. Stevie had kept his wits about him and exited the barrel just twenty yards before the fence. For some reason, after making a cool clear eyed decision like that, he had decided to lay down and take a nap. I figured he was waiting for help to roll the barrel back up the hill. I nudged him and when he woke up, he acted silly and couldn't crawl straight. I couldn't wait for my turn.

The experience from inside the barrel is far different. It's like watching an old reel movie with the frames flashing by. Sky-grass-sky-grass-sky-grass... repeat thirty thousand times. It's interesting, as the mind's focus turns from enjoying a new experience toward one of surviving a frantic ordeal. As the frames merged into a blue-green blur, I hit the ski jump. It took Stevie only thirty seconds to get to the ski jump on his ride. On my ride, it took an hour and a half. I had forgotten about it, so going airborne was a complete surprise. The instant relief from the pounding of terrain was accentuated by the weightlessness of flight. Gravity pays back what gets stolen, and the earth rose to punch the barrel with astonishing force. I made the mistake of concentrating on the grass whipping my face with every turn as my head was hanging out the open end of the barrel. Distracted, I forgot to bail out like Stevie before reaching the fence. The arresting net caught me, but I was trapped.

After a while, it got hot in the barrel. I managed to rock the barrel and squeeze out through the barbed wire with minor scratches. Stevie was nowhere to be found. Laying in the blessedly cool grass the clouds spun. A grasshopper landed on my face and his prickly feet on my cheek was not enough bother to raise a hand to sweep him away. The wind sounded nice in the grass. I decided to take a nap.

I awoke and re-discovered myself lying in the pasture next to a paper barrel. The cows had managed to join me in the thick cool grass during the heat of the day, lying around, chewing their cud. The paper barrel had some scars on it and not just a few grass stains. It would be better back in the barn before dad noticed. God is not that complicated. Hills are for going down.

The Road

I had acquired a used red American Flyer bicycle built for the rugged rigors of youth. My brother Stevie had a similar bike, a used red Schwinn. If the automobile extended American's freedom to explore and discover the country, the bicycle was the warmup act for kids.

We had been limited to riding on rough trails in the pasture, through the orchard, and around the lawn. Perhaps the areas of dirt track we had worn into the lawn around the corners of the house raised the possibility. Perhaps it was the selective pruning of certain trees in the orchard that resulted in better times for our obstacle course. Perhaps it was having the cattle "surprised" by something a few times too often that caused them to run through the pasture fences. But the day came when we were allowed to explore the rest of the universe and ride our bikes on the road.

We lived in an area experimenting with development. It was not at the edge of the city, but not in the midst of big farms either. We could look across the back-property line at big farms, but up and down our road were neighbors with large lots and small acreages, playing with country living. Farms had been carved up along the road to allow more neighbors. Some raised sheep and calves, some had small orchards. There was a widow with just a garden, a commercial chicken farmer, and a guy who just mowed a lot of grass. There was a neighbor with a giant machine shed and a trucking business. The road tied us to the city at one end of our universe, and to the giant grain farms at the other.

We lived at a bend in the road. There was no reason for the road to bend, except our house was in the way. If you went straight through, and down a hill with a sixty-foot vertical drop, you would line right up and connect with the road going east again. Instead, the road veered north, went around a few neighbors' properties, and reconnected with itself going east. Our hill was too much for the road. Like daring a neighbor kid to ride his bike over the edge, the road chickened out and snaked around the skirt of the hill.

Our normal trips were limited to the familiar part of the road, to the city and back, and to the north bend and back. This was the neighborhood for us. It stretched three miles and was home for a dozen families. There was the old widow who shared a party line for the phone with us. She would stop us as we rode by and ask us about family things we thought no one knew about. Next to her was the professional gardener. He raised mysterious crops behind the house, but the entire front yard was a giant garden. If he was tending his garden, we were welcome to stop and taste things. We learned things, too. There were good bugs and bad bugs, plants used just for making food taste good and plants used for healing. We learned lots and didn't mind a bit.

The sheep farmer was a little cool to us. It may have been because we found the sheep so fun to scare. He lived on the inside corner of the road with a sheep pasture between the road and his house. We would scope out the premises for human activity before starting our fun. Stevie hid at the corner to one side of the pasture. I settled at the adjacent side. One of us would start by jumping out of the tall grass mimicking a wild predator on the attack. The sheep, fleeing to the farthest end of their containment only found another frantic predator jumping out of the ditch in full howling attack. They would turn as a school of fish in perfect coordinated motion flashing their wooly coats over a blur of black legs. Back and forth until the herd was nestled against the corner furthest from the road and nearest the house, bleating their worried calls. I suppose all the running made them hungry.

Adventure lay down the road in every direction. When we turned our bicycles from the driveway to the road, we followed its wheels to any whim.

Our road was a gravel road, far superior to a mere dirt road. After a rain, the gravel would get packed into the softened clay beneath it, and dried to make hard smooth tire lanes. At times, we could speed with ease along these prepared strips until a car would come along and push us back to slogging it through loose gravel on the edges.

If we went west, we only had one steep hill and one long hill before reaching the edge of the city. The road stopped at the edge of the city joining a proper paved intersection in a quiet neighborhood. Here, the houses sat within arms-reach of one another. This is where neighbors could smell each other's cooking, hear each other's music, and know each other's business. As country kids, we were afraid of the city. We probed the first block or two of smooth paved city streets before scampering back to the road. Years later I was astonished to learn that city kids were afraid of the country, and would stop at the gravel road, and look out into the countryside at the unknown dangers that lay out there.

When we went north, the road would bend itself east again. But at the bend a little dirt road peeled off to the northwest. The dirt road was a mystery. We had no idea where it went once it was swallowed up by trees in the valley. Our imaginations filled in what the lack of facts and experience couldn't. We imagined and told tales about the kind of people who lived in the hidden valley down the dirt road. Crazy demented people doing secret experiments. Places where kids would be lost and never returned. Criminals on the run, cattle rustlers, and bank robbers hiding out until the heat was off. The greater the stories became, the more we dared one another to go in. That day came.

Upon entering, the dirt road climbed to a brief crest then descended into the hidden valley. Stevie and I probed the threshold. After a few short skirmishes down the dirt road, it was time to breach the tree lined valley. The first mile connected a few little farms tucked into hollows between hills, set well back off their little dirt road. It was far enough. While we had seen nothing strange, we had seen enough to confirm our suspicions and continue our stories.

We continued back to the safe proximity of the road. Stevie and I loitered over the crest circling our bikes on the dirt road. We were having fun hitting pockets of dry powdered clay that had settled in pot holes. They burst like land mines as dust bombs that hung in the still summer air of the valley. A pickup truck sprang over the crest, surprising us, like a fox on a hen napping on a nest. We hadn't been watching, and our escape route was sealed off. With no choice, we made a mad dash on our bikes deeper into the valley pursued by the rusty old red truck bearing down on us. Building speed on the dirt road going into the valley, we kept ahead of the beast. We heard it grinding its gears, and a fresh roar from the engine. A sinister squealing came from under its hood. A quick look back, and the truck was galloping over potholes, raising an impenetrable smoke screen of powdered clay in its wake. The rusty old truck pressed its limit as its mad smiling driver bore down on us, salivating over the impending capture. We managed to hold our lead through the twisting levels deeper in the secret valley. We had never traveled this far, pushed as we were, by a demented old hermit. Around a fresh bend, we saw a long rise and knew that somewhere along its length we would be overcome and face our destiny. It would be best not to look and just push the bike pedals hard and fast until our legs cramped and the truck would chew us up under its axles. But with our lungs burning and our legs shaking, we looked back, expecting our assailant to be looming. He hadn't made the last bend! Across the valley, through the trees, we saw him ambling down a long driveway past piles of weathered junk toward a ramshackle house. He had given up! We out ran the old goat and would live to tell the tale to the neighbor kids!

Taking the road around the north bend and going east was reserved for our long adventures. The road climbed alongside and up a set of hills for another mile, making its way to the crest of a ridge. Starting from its damp grassy bottom where the crickets chirped night and day, the road climbed to fields, and wind, and sun. It rose to grand views of the adjoining valleys. We could look back at the home place along its length, so the distance never stretched beyond the subconscious limits of our safe playground. After an arduous climb to the peak we would turn our bikes around and look down upon its falling length beneath our tires. Waiting while our hearts pounded to a rate slow enough to speak, we passed on conversation and let the wind fill our ears. We savored the solid minutes of downhill gliding. Downhill on a bike is a solitary experience. Only the road, the wind, and the feel of machinery getting beaten by gravel and pot-holes. Half way down, old lady Simpson's dog would chase us and on occasion snag a tooth on a pant leg. Once entangled he flipped and rolled over the edge of the road into the ditch. We never saw him on the ascent, but he enjoyed our rapid descent as much as we did. The persistent danger of hitting a soft gravel patch and landing in the ditch heightened the pulse.

Then tired, dusty, with new tales to tell, we followed the road home. The road. New boundaries. New fears. A new universe.

Fear

"Hello little soul. Attained some wisdom yet?"

"I am learning about freedom and choices, and how to extend my boundaries."

"I've been watching. Quite a time down there with old Ben Nelson. You know he was having a good time giving you a chase. What are you learning as you stretch your limits?"

"I guess it's always a bit scary, but once I've gone somewhere, it seems OK. Even after learning that, the next mile is scary again."

"The great unknown. Almost never a problem. Fear holds people back. Fear is a test. People fear unknown lands. They fear one another. They fear tomorrow. But fear is a test of faith. Overcoming fear, to experience something new, is to practice faith."

"But God, some take chances and fail. They get hurt. I watch them withdraw. It's too much to keep trying. Or sometimes, when I try new things, people will lecture and scold."

"As despair teaches about love, fear teaches about faith. As a soul, you know I have a most exquisite eternity waiting. And yet you fear much. Would it not be logical, knowing the glory of your ultimate destiny, to take great risks for sheer adventure? Many wait for their time to pass, making no effort, taking no chance. They fear the end of their lives too. But I made you to be afraid and have doubts, so you could find faith. In finding it, working for it, testing it, it becomes valuable. As you discover faith, you will one day look forward to your destiny with anticipation and even excitement."

"Is that why grandma laughs at things that upset mom and dad?"

God chuckled, "Indeed your grandma understands. She has come to know Me and thus has little fear. Her journey as a widow is just about over. Those grand old souls without fear get little notice, but they are wells of wisdom."

"Mom complains to dad that grandma is undermining our upbringing."

"Your mother has great fear : worldly concerns of raising a family, maintaining a reputation, having resources, daily chores of all types. She feels responsible for how her kids behave and grow up and join society. She's afraid if your dad dies she will be a penniless widow. These are good concerns to have at this point of her adventure. She cannot see Me or understand Me because of her fear."

"But she's a good church going person!"

"Yes, she is. For now, church gives her soul a guide rope to her purpose. I know her soul has a firm grip on that rope as your mother has many worries. She's sleeping now. I just visited with her."

"How can she obey the rules and go to church but not see you?"

"You complain yourself how you seem so distant during your waking moments. Your days can be confused by people providing answers that are not mine. For the price of submission they deliver fear and seize power. Follow the rules and stay out of trouble. Join the group or face exclusion. That struggle can last a lifetime. Faith is shaken over and again by fear. I am asking you to search for great faith.

"Many around you preach fear. Fear of

loneliness, pain, discomfort. Can they protect you? Can they heal you? Do you give them your faith? Do you follow the insecure to bolster their egos? Show no fear and watch them go elsewhere.

"Your mother's soul is just like you, hanging on, seeking me out, being refreshed. Her soul brushes her memory, snuggles her heart, and puts her feet on the ground. As a soul you can overcome the fear your waking mind can't. You can be the source of faith you need."

The Cistern

The Aeromotor wind mill once numbered over 100,000 across the great plains. From the Dakotas to Texas the Great Plains are windy more often than not. A typical Aeromotor system would be built whereby the windmill ran a pump that would lift water to a cistern to be stored for when the wind took a rest. When the cistern was full, you could drop a lever to turn the windmill out of the wind and shut it off. We had a main cistern up by the house, and a second, smaller cistern down by the barn for the animals.

Our old cistern was still in operation, even though electricity had come to the farm before I was born. Dad was a stickler about turning the lights off because electricity had to be paid for. Extending the logic, it was clear, there was no point in paying to pump water. The cistern was an underground concrete tank of some mysterious depth that would hold enough water to last between long dry spells without wind.

Like a lot of things on the farm, the cistern had the potential to be another way to die. The top of our cistern was covered by a raised wooden box, with one board left unfastened. Every so often, during a hot muggy spell without wind, Dad would lift the loose board, dip a long skinny stick way down into the tank, and see how much watcr was left. We wouldn't have to take baths again until the wind blew. Mom and us boys would say prayers about the weather for opposite reasons for a while. It was against the rules to take the loose board off because the cistern was deep and the sides were straight and smooth. If you fell in, you would drown and die, and the water would go bad until you had fully rotted away. Of course, we would lift the board off, sneak a look, consider our gruesome deaths in the cistern, and back away.

The wood box on the cistern was the spot where dad and grandpa would sit and talk. Grandpa would smoke Lucky Strikes, and I suppose he was not allowed to do so in the house. As such, the cistern became the men's spot to solve the world's problems. We'd sit on dad or grandpa's knee and listen. They would talk about the railroad, the crops, the animals, cars and trucks, and good stuff like that. Grandpa and dad liked to talk about how things worked and what great new stuff the world was coming up with.

The cistern was also the spot where we kids learned how to gamble. There were a variety of card games the family enjoyed. Sometimes dad would sit on a corner of the cistern, and us kids would kneel in the dirt around the sides and play cards. That was where Dad taught us blackjack. The ante was a penny, and the maximum bet was five cents. Fifty cents was the maximum loss, which was a weeks' allowance. Dad would whip us and take our money. He was teaching us lessons about taking risk and absorbing losses. While he was as kind hearted as they come about everything else in life, he always kept our gambling losses. He would say, "You know how that feels? Some day when you need that money to buy milk and bread it will feel worse."

Of course, we thought playing blackjack, gambling, and taking each other's money was pretty cool. Losing didn't feel half as bad compared to how much winning your brother's allowance felt good. I suspect we were not picking up on life's lessons all that fast. We lost many weeks' allowances around that cistern. We spent a particular summer's evening swapping change, and we kids were winning. Dad's heart was not in it that night. The next morning was Sunday, and normally dad could be counted on to read the funnies to us. It was the nice kind of morning that you forget. Sunny, dew damp, and cool. It felt good to be cold because you knew the day would be hot. Dad was out sitting on the cistern which was odd. I walked outside in my pajamas and asked dad why he was sitting outside in the morning. Grandpa had died the night before. Dad looked lonely, but I had a strange feeling that Grandpa was sitting there with him.

Uncles and neighbors would come out and sit on the cistern. There was talk about the state trying to run a lottery that would rake in lots of money, pay all the bills, and lower taxes. One night, our neighbor, Jack, asked my dad, "Merle, they say a man could buy a ticket for a dollar and walk home with a million in one pop. What would you do if you won that kind of money?"

Dad thought about it for a few seconds and said, "Well I suppose I'd just farm 'til it was gone." It sounded like the lottery was a lot like gambling, but way better than farming.

Years went by, but we still sat on the cistern on long summer evenings. At some point mom objected to periods of teenage boys stinking up the house on hot summer days without bathing. A new well was dug with an electric pump installed. The windmill was hauled off by a scrap dealer. But the cistern still sat there, an empty cement hole under the aging wooden platform, and we still sat on it. The planks were getting rotten and there was no point in fixing it. But it was becoming dangerous. A plan was crafted. The cistern would have to go, and a fancy new deck to sit on would be built. Dad saw an opportunity.

About twice a month, the accumulated garbage around the farm would be loaded up in the pickup truck and hauled off to the dump. Once loaded, we kids would pile in, squeezed across a bench seat or sitting on laps with windows rolled down. Dump day was a treat because we had to go through "rolley coaster hills" to get there. In this part of Iowa, the melting glaciers had cut the Missouri river floodplain, but had also deposited great steep hills and bluffs on either side of the river. Before giant road building equipment came along to slice through hills and make straight and level paths, roads simply followed the contours of terrain, rising and dropping with whatever hill happened to be beneath them. Back in the county where the landfill operated, there was a road going through a set of hills that was put down by billy goats instead of road engineers.

The dusty gravel road went past a remote farm. Dad said the lucky farmer was getting paid rent for ten years to have a dump. When it was done, he'd have a whole valley filled in with forty acres of nice level farmland on top. He merely had to put up with the stench for ten years. Man, he was a lucky farmer. He got everybody's junk. Lots of bad stuff, but good stuff, too. Sometimes at the dump we'd look over the piles, pointing out the terrible waste, but dad wouldn't let us bring any of it home. Pot belly stoves, chunks of lumber, bicycles better than our own. Glass and metal, cans and jars. A terrible waste, but we were betting the farmer would sneak out at night and grab most of the good stuff before it got buried.

Entering rolley coaster hills started with the climb up the first hill. Dad would gun the engine of the old truck and get some speed going. Popping over the top, the wheels would leave the ground and our stomachs would lift into our throats. We'd lift off the seats and float while the truck carried us forward over the crest. The truck would land and push us into the seats, or down into the lap we were sitting on. There would be screams and laughter. Coming down the hill the truck would gain even more speed, making a good run up the next higher hill. More squeals as the truck would shimmy in spots with loose gravel under the tires, and then we were airborne again. A moment of silence as we experienced artificially induced highs. There were screams and groans and belly laughs recovering from the second landing. But a moment later we returned to terrified stares out the windshield careening down the ramp to the third hill.

This run had a longer approach, and dad used every bit to build speed. The last hill was the big one. If you didn't gain enough speed going up, it would be a dud. I think dad worried sometimes about making it over the hill. The road was only a lane and a half wide and someone else may barrel over the top. Sweat would drip off his nose, unnoticed, his eyes forward. Going up we looked straight out the windshield into the blue sky above. We never left the ground or lost our stomachs going over the top on the last hill. The fun was from the near vertical climb followed by the near vertical drop on the other side. As we rolled over the crest, our faces would be planted on the windshield, holding us back as we stared down the narrow gravel path right to the bottom with nothing in our way. Dad would shift the truck into low gear, and the engine would scream like an airplane coming down the slope for a landing at the bottom.

The dump had a unique and awful smell. It was rotten, dusty, metallic, and wet. The smell was so strong you could taste it. You could feel it crawling on your skin, just beneath the flies.

The truck would back up to the pile, and we'd all jump out. While dad threw the garbage into the edge of the pile, we admired the man driving the caterpillar. He would drive the big CAT right up into the pile of garbage and push it over the edge until he almost went over into the ravine below. Sometimes he'd go so far over the top we could only see the smoke from his engine. We thought he was a dead goner, rolling the big machine down into the valley. It was exciting.

The dry clay soil would swirl into little dust devils and mix with the smells and lighter floating bits of garbage. We could chase them if we stayed away from the big CAT. A great swarm of birds would announce us, circling and landing, screeching and taking off again. They were fat birds, living off the garbage, flies, and mosquitoes. The dump was a visceral experience for the raw senses of children.

On hot summer days, we'd be all dusty, and sweaty, and smell like a dump, and get back into the truck for the return ride over rolley coaster hills. The return ride would be more fun and less stressful because dad didn't have to worry about losing a load of garbage out the back. Once we cleared the big hill, it was all about speed, losing our stomachs, and catching a little air under the tires. Dad was pretty conservative, except on dump days.

The decommissioned cistern sat there like an unused ballistic missile silo. The plan was to commit to spring cleaning and throw everything into the old cistern. Every room in the house, the basement, the barn, the garage, was scoured for junk. Old bicycles and buckets and brooms. Old clothes and sewing machines and rugs. Toys, radios, baseball cards, and Sunbeam appliances went in there. Chunks of farm equipment, fence posts, and old barbed wire. We cleaned and tossed, and cleaned and tossed for a month. When we had thrown out everything we could think of to part with, we tore off the rotted old platform.

It turned out we could have taken our baths. Whoever built the cistern must have been very thirsty at some time in their life. We looked down into a watery cavern twelve feet in diameter. A quiet pool of water, still eight feet down below the edge hid the junk resting at some mysterious depth. Most small towns had water towers with less capacity than our cistern. No one ever knew how big or deep it was. Dad put the front-end loader on the tractor and went to work. He moved dirt all day to fill in our time capsule.

The cistern was covered over, and a layer of gravel went on top. Above it Dad built a deck longer and wider than the house. I suppose, as we sat on the deck, we were still sitting on the old cistern. We talked about the weather, and animals, and hills, and God. I think there were moments I heard Grandpa in the conversation as well.

Grandma

Sunday morning found us heading for church and stopping on the way to pick up Grandma. Mom, Dad, and Suzy sat in front of the big old Mercury, so grandma would slide in the back with the rest of us kids. Grandma always had a funny smell. Not that it bothered us. Growing up on a farm, we were swallowed up in smells. Rich, fermenting aromas. Manure soaked hay that the dog would dig in, rotting fruit to pick up in the orchard, wedges of cabbage baking with mom's roast. We knew the smells of oil soaked dirt on the machine shed floor, wet dogs, and newborn calves. Earthy, living smells. Grandma was just one of these. It might have been her hair. She always wore her hair knotted up in a bun on top of her head, held together with bobby pins and hair spray. Or maybe her old coat that hung in the closet with the mothballs. Or maybe it was something else.

Having Grandma along meant a stop after church for breakfast at the café next to the Sunshine grocery store. Grandma lived alone now, and I think she enjoyed the banter around the table. Conversations could move from cartoons to politics to something on a cereal box. The arrival of pancakes and bacon limited the conversation to the adults.

Proudly displayed on the front counter of the café was an automated donut maker. The latest in mechanized technology, the sides were made of glass so crowds could gather and watch. The donut machine launched a ring of dough onto a slow-moving stream of boiling oil. Sizzling and browning on the bottoms, the tops bubbled. About halfway across, they would stop at a barrier, and a wire rack appeared from below to lift them up and flip them over. We absorbed the aromas of hot cooking oil and frying donuts, fresh coffee, and frying bacon. Gears spun, chains looped, racks moved, dough squirted. As the donuts reached the end of their voyage, another wire flipped them out of the boiling river and down a steel chute. Sugared while still wet and warm, hand frosted, or just plain, we took six donuts back to the table for our breakfast desert.

After breakfast, we helped grandma do her grocery shopping. Peppered by advertising between cartoons, we practiced our mind washing. Hey, grandma! Get Roasty's peanut butter because it smells more like real peanuts! She made gracious excuses, without explaining that peanut butter would pull her false teeth off, but always seemed interested in our little sales pitch.

Every so often my brother and I slept over at grandma's house. I suppose the girls did too, but we never heard from them. Mom or Dad would suggest a sleepover on the way home from church at a moment Grandma might exhibit a weakness. If she mentioned no one had been by to see her, dad would chip in, "Well, why don't we let the boys sleep over for a night. That will liven things up." Somehow, our bags were already packed in the trunk.

After an afternoon of exploring Grandma's gardens, garages, basement and attic, we were fed, bathed and played cards. At bed-time we ran up the corner staircase. There were two rooms upstairs, a small one grandma slept in, and a bigger one with two beds. On one side was the hospital style bed that grandpa stayed in while he was sick before he died. We would dare each other to sit on it, then wonder if Grandpa was watching and if his ghost would come back to spank us.

Across the room was the big sleigh bed in which we slept. It was so big you could sleep sideways or crooked, or any way you wanted, and never know what direction you were sleeping until morning. The bed was against one wall. With the huge headboard and footboard, it formed a three sided box. Grandma tucked us in and turned out the light. For a while we laid in the dark and talked about ghosts as sleep crept upon us.

I was awakened by an eerie wailing. Scared, I sat up, and heard Stevie's muffled screams from somewhere in the dark. "Where are you?" I shouted. Screams commenced. I figured Stevie was somewhere over by the screams, and I sure didn't want to go over there. Whatever had him might get me, too. Logic prevailed, and I tried to get out of bed by running the other way. "Bam", right into a wall. Somehow, there were walls encircling the bed, and I couldn't escape. Continuing to apply Vulcan-like logic, I beat on the wall and screamed.

With some passage of time equal to development of a hoarseness from screaming, a light on the ceiling appeared. I looked around in the misty-eyed vapor of midnight. The ghost of Benjamin Franklin appeared under the light bulb on the ceiling. He was wearing a white robe and had long white flowing hair with a bald head. He wore little wire rim spectacles, and when he went to speak he had no teeth! Being of sound mental material, I turned and ran up the high headboard of the sleigh bed and perched on top against the corner of the wall.

I heard grandma's voice, "What is going on?", and I saw that grandma had somehow vanquished the ghost of Benjamin Franklin when she entered the room. She also had a white robe and a bald head! She stood there, adjusting her false teeth with a tired stern look crossing her face.

"Stevie's gone." And sure enough, at the mention of his voice, Stevie's screams began again. Grandma looked toward the foot of the bed, and I crawled over to see. Somehow Stevie was rolled up in a blanket and wedged between the mattress and the footboard. His face was smashed over against one side, but you could see both of his terrified eyes looking up at us. Grandma pried him loose and pulled him out. She tucked us back in without comment. Lights were out, and grandma sighed as she closed the door. We spent time laying there, discussing how much grandma looked like Ben Franklin, and wondering if Grandpa's ghost had shoved Stevie into the footboard for bouncing on his bed.

For some reason, Dad came over early to pick us up the next day. He asked us if we had a good time sleeping over and if there was any trouble. Everything was fine, except we would have to tell mom how we ripped Stevie's pajamas on the lift machine that worked Grandpa's bed. We were wondering if you buried canned peaches in a floor drain if a tree would grow in Grandma's basement. And we probably left the tire swing on the porch roof. But otherwise it was a good sleepover. Dad smiled. He seemed well rested.

Uncle Ted

In the Missouri river valley, between the river and backed up against the hills, is a low spot. A simple accident of nature, produced as the glaciers melted and a great flow of water forty miles wide made its way south to the Gulf of Mexico. By the turn of a hill, a protruding stone, a washed-up log, or a drifted sand bar, the flow swirled and produced an undercurrent. A crescent-shaped low spot a hundred yards at the widest, and maybe five times that long, now flooded by the river, and refreshed by water flowing through the sand bars. One end was still connected and open to the river, and the other tapered off to a sandy shallow beach. A pleasant little backwater, called Ox Horn lake, alongside which Uncle Ted and Auntie Lue kept a little house.

Uncle Ted and Auntie Lue would make their way to our farm on occasion, but more often we ventured to them and their whimsical little spot on Ox Horn lake. Dotted with bird feeders, and squirrel feeders, and deer feeders, and even a worm farm, creation seemed content at this locale. Uncle Ted was retired from the railroad and was glad to watch us kids for an afternoon when the folks got too busy. Auntie Lue would smile and greet us with cookies. She was tall but round in most parts, giving evidence to her skills in the kitchen.

Stevie and I were deposited one morning after

swimming lessons to spend the day. Auntie Lue fed us and warmed us up. Uncle Ted sat in a rocking chair, smoking a pipe next to a massive field-stone fireplace surrounded by an eclectic collection of statues and planted pots. Auntie Lue nourished the brier of tropical plants and embellished them with tigers, snakes, and an elephant poking between the ferns and vines. A strange African themed room along a bend in the river in Iowa. Our imaginations loved a compelling jungle.

Uncle Ted spoke without looking up from his paper, "It's a nice morning. You boys want to learn how to fish?" And while we figured we knew how to fish, we also figured Uncle Ted was going to teach us something. We nodded vigorously with our mouths still savoring cookies and cocoa.

Uncle Ted's garage had neat collections of useful things in quantities beyond need. There was the fortress wall of empty coffee cans. There was the home built wooden rack groaning under stacks of used electric motors, salvaged from fans, vacuum cleaners, mixers, and well pumps. There was a neat collection of fishing rods, dangling by cup hooks across half the ceiling. Uncle Ted walked us to a corner. "Your folks called and said you were coming, so I mixed up some bait last night." Pointing to a bucket, "Those are chicken livers. I soaked 'em overnight in vinegar and sorghum. They should be good and ripe by now. Back here on the lake we need to attract the fish to come up out of the river. We need some good and stinky bait that will send scent downstream and get the fish to come investigate." While we personally preferred fresh meat in our diets, it made perfect sense to us that fish would prefer fermented bits of rotted liver.

Ted showed us how to bait the hooks and cast the lines. Then, instead of sitting by the water, we reeled off thirty extra yards of line and walked our rods back to the porch. There we sat in the shade on uneven rocking chairs wearing the paint off the porch floor and sipping Dr. Peppers. Ted knew how to fish. "You see, the fish are down there in the river and it will take a while for them to smell our bait. So, I like to sit here where it's comfortable and wait." And we did. We talked and laughed. Auntie Lue joined us, served us lemonade, and laughed with us, too. They teased us about girls we didn't like yet, the teachers we probably did, and hobbies we probably shouldn't. Ted was resting his Dr. Pepper on a bit of a beer belly and saw us looking at him. "You know the doctor says this is a serious case." The twinkle in his eye betrayed his serious voice. "Yup, I'm pregnant. First case like this he's seen in a while." And Auntie Lue laughed. Ted went on, "And it's a baby elephant." Perplexed and chuckling we took-the-bait and asked how it could be an elephant. "Well the doctor looked, and he knows it's a baby elephant because his trunk is already hanging out." We rolled on the porch in uncontrollable fits. Auntie Lue laughed too, then scolded Ted for corrupting us, and went in to make lunch.

Time passed, and Auntie Lue died. She was Dad's older sister by ten years, so Stevie and I were doing the math on Dad's likely departure date while sitting in church waiting for the funeral to start. Funerals were a lot like weddings, but also different. The whole family came and said the things they should and a few they shouldn't. The ladies dressed in black dresses and wore white lace on their heads. People were talking in church, just loud enough to be heard, but just soft enough to deny it. People sat where they wanted to, but no one sat up front by the casket.

Ted was gracious but wet eyed welcoming people as they entered the church. He shook people's hands and smiled between tears. The body was displayed, and Auntie Lue looked well for a dead person. The Priest said nice things about Auntie Lue and they were all true. He was reassuring and almost cheerful at the prospect of Auntie Lue joining the souls in heaven.

It was a nice summer day, and we joined the caravan of cars to the cemetery. While it was not far, we got to drive through a couple of red lights, and oncoming traffic pulled over and stopped for us. A thunderstorm the night before had left the day fresh and clear. The grave site service was muffled by the breeze in the trees, the songbirds, the crickets, and the ducks in the nearby pond. The casket was suspended over a deep rectangular hole in the ground, and a tarp covered the pile of dirt next to it. Stevie and I wanted to hang around afterward to see them scoop the dirt in, but we were nudged to the car. Dinner followed in the church basement and the communal conversation continued.

Dad's sisters recalled things from too long ago to remember. Mom cried and laughed and Dad sat with his brother Herb and Uncle Ted and drank beer from long necked brown bottles. When we went home, we felt good about Auntie Lue. She would be waiting for us in heaven, and it was good to know there would be someone nice there that we already knew.

Three weeks later, Uncle Ted was found dead.

Mom took the phone call and gasped and listened. “Suicide,” Mom said, “In his garage.” Dad came home early that day. Mom had made macaroni and cheese early, and hustled us off to watch TV, while she and Dad had dinner alone. Bed time came before sunset, and Stevie and I sat up on our beds, looked out our window at the lengthening shadows, and wondered about Ted.

Without the details, we were carried along to a different kind of funeral. We met at Uncle Ted’s house with just a few relatives. “Why is there no priest? Why is there no funeral?” Mom told us our cousins had asked the priest what he would say, but he wouldn’t say anything nice, so they decided not to have a church funeral. “But Ted was the nicest guy ever.” We were told to shush and not say anything inappropriate.

The cousins had Uncle Ted cremated. The extended family gathered around and stood by the shore of Ox Horn lake. Each cousin read a remembrance of Uncle Ted . The oldest cousin took the urn with ashes and slung the contents toward the lake. Most of the ashes drifted back across the onlookers. Stevie and I giggled at an inappropriate moment but we refrained from saying what occurred to us. A few chunks splashed in the water. We wondered about the fish.

The cousins had set up a buffet of sandwiches in the house. Pictures of Uncle Ted and Auntie Lue were set behind the table, looking just like they did a month before. We sat on the back porch next to Ox Horn lake, on the rocking chairs, and wore a little more paint off the floor. The aunts were dismayed because Ted’s soul was going to burn in hell for eternity for taking his own life. We kids were to learn lessons from this. One of the cousins explained that Ted had loved Auntie Lue so much that he had gotten depressed and decided he couldn't live without her. The arm chair religion went on for a while as heaven and hell were anything but a decided convention.

And after blaming themselves, the church, the doctors, and the neighbors the extended family disbursed. We turned and left the cousins in the driveway, waving a long goodbye. It took a long time to go to sleep that night.

His Will be Done

"Looking for someone?" God said.

"Yes, we had a disturbing funeral this week. Ted was a great guy, but all my aunts were convinced he was going to hell for killing himself."

"I know. People like rules for behavior. They're not always sure where danger lies, so they like rules that will keep them safe. They have created lots of rules that will send people to hell."

"Well, are they right?"

"Oh! Yes sometimes people do need their rules to behave better."

"No, I mean about Uncle Ted!"

"I know, I'm toying with you! Let me ask you, did Ted hate me? Did he rail against me and take people away from their holy purpose in life?"

"Of course not! Ted was the friendliest person you'd ever meet. He went to church, and treated people well, and was always the kind of person who helped folks out. Sometimes he had a knack for telling people just the right thing at just the right time."

"Yes, Ted and I had a bit of a connection at times."

"So, Ted's in heaven?"

"Yes, of course. I made heaven and earth and all things. I am capable of deciding where souls spend eternity. People like to define and limit what my abilities are. Pure silliness sometimes. I create matter and it obeys me. I create time and it obeys me. I create consciousness and by my command give it free will to create and think and experiment. Yes, I am quite

capable of bringing a soul back to heaven."

"Somehow I knew that."

"Yes, you already did. You should listen to yourself more often!"

"And when will I discover my soul and listen to it?"

"Every time you think of Me. Every time you contemplate. When you are quiet. These are the times you open avenues to understanding. Press on your waking self even more and watch yourself grow! You are almost old enough to understand. One of these days, you are going to have an awakening moment, and begin to think! You will choose more of your steps. You will decide how to complete your purpose.

"Maybe you will bury your fear and take a risk. You might choose peace and joy. You might choose a great work. In the end, you know I will bring you home."

Dust Motes

Dust motes defy gravity. I woke up lying on a pillow and blanket on the living room floor. The bedrooms upstairs would not cool off on muggy August nights. After lying awake for a while I would slide down the stairs in the dark on my bottom, one step at a time, with bedding in tow. Morning would find Stevie and I and sometimes the girls curled up like pets in a corner, somewhere cool and quiet. This particular morning a sunbeam was exposed by dust motes. It was drawing a line from the corner of the window across the room to where it covered half a family picture on the wall. The light erased a diagonal slice of the photo in glare, with the remaining half a gathering smiling in the shadow. With no reason to move, I lay there and watched it for a while. One could not see the light beam, but the tiny bits of dust resting in the air reflected and shimmered themselves into a golden beam.

I could hear the chickens stirring in the distance. Dad was up doing chores. He'd come in to fry eggs soon, and if I got up he'd make one for me too. Breakfast all by myself with dad was infrequent but nice. It was special in a plain way. "Ya want an egg? A hard one or a messy one?" And we'd chat in soft tones so no one would wake up. For most of breakfast, we didn't say much. "Nice morning, but it's gonna be hot. You kids have swimming lessons today? I want the windfalls in the orchard picked up. I'll see ya tonight."

A hug and back to the floor with a pillow. He'd go off to work for someone else all day.

Dad usually drove a truck during the day. Sometimes he worked in the office at the pipeline. But mostly he would get a truck filled with gasoline and deliver it to gas stations. Just an ordinary thing to do that no one noticed. He and mom ran a small farm. Like a million other farmers, nothing notable was going on.

When dad came home that night, he left after dinner. There was a meeting of the neighboring farmers. Farmers didn't see each other much. A nod here and there at church, an evening watching kids at school events. The town gatherings for Independence Day and Christmas wrapped up the opportunities for conversation. A meeting was rare.

We learned that Frank, a neighbor down the road was in the hospital getting an operation, and he wouldn't be able to feed his animals or farm for a month. Frank was a real farmer. He had two hundred acres of corn and pasture and fed a hundred calves. His only son was away at the seminary. The neighbors set up a plan to take turns feeding Franks cattle. A week later the neighbors went to Franks' farm, and the men and boys baled hay. One mother organized the kids with chores to help-out for the day. Frank sat on his porch and watched his neighbors keep his farm in order. Frank recovered, and no one mentioned it again. No great lesson was preached. It was an ordinary thing.

Great ordinary things happened all the time. Dust motes defy gravity.

Bits of Dust

"Why are we so insignificant?" the little soul was petulant sitting at the edge. "There are billions of us. There are magnificent landscapes, wondrous creatures, beautiful fauna, oceans and lands. Yet I am but a dust mote in the universe! Stars and galaxies beyond count. You are God beyond imagination and wonder. But if I am to journey through my adventure with purpose why am I so insignificant?"

"Let's examine this universe, my little soul. Look upon that giant redwood tree. Magnificent creature, yes? What is it made of?"

"I guess leaves, bark, and wood. Water and sap I suppose."

"What are those components made of?"

"Cells, molecules, atoms I guess."

"Such is everything. The most significant things of the physical universe I created, are composed of the most insignificant bits of dust. Atoms build molecules, molecules build cells, and cells build branches in to trees. Do you see my pattern? People copy it in their organizations. In their machines. In their commerce. They build great things from small parts."

"But dear God, I am unique and wish to do great things. Am I not as capable as any other soul to make a serious impact from my journey?"

"My Son once told a tale, still often repeated. It was about a farmer who hired workers throughout the day. At the end of the day all the workers were paid the same amount. The story is often misunderstood in human context. He was making it clear that all of

heaven was available to all souls no matter how large or small their purpose on earth was. If you lived one minute or a hundred years, all of heaven would be yours. While the trunk of the tree is impressive, and the leaves are beautiful, it cannot exist without roots and sap, or without the tiny bits that make it work.

"Yes, you are unique. Because of that you are important. Your journey will bring another element to heaven one day. Your job is to make the most of what you are given. Go out to give and receive. Do not fear, and you will find more."

"But I remain trivial. What can I do to change any of this? The world does not see me, nor will it miss me."

"Perhaps. You seem focused on the physical world. The universe is a grand creation. Look close at an insect and see the perfection in all its parts. From the fine hairs to the luminescent colors. Quite nice. Then look through a telescope at the galaxies and the vicious wheels of creation moving in timeframes that span thousands of human lives. And perhaps you feel small. But think again. What of the physical universe? It is but bits of one kind of dust repeated many times, in many patterns. One bit done over and over. A simple set of protons and electrons, spun and organized in millions of different patterns, but still just the same bits of dust.

"Now think some more about the non-physical universe. These are the creations, inventions, and compositions of the soul. Not one bit, but billions of ethereal creations.

"If a man is banished and he dies from exposure, the elements will strip his flesh and grind his bones back to dust. In his life, he experienced suffering and joy, love and pain. He enjoyed a good sermon, tasted

good food, created thoughts, and shared ideas. These are the gifts he brings to heaven. They are unique without physical form or substance. There is nothing of the physical world with meaning in heaven other than the one small bit it is made of.

"Whether composed or heard, what does music mean to the physical universe?

"What does creative thought and invention mean other than to bend the soil to purpose?

"Stories are written and read. Emotion is felt.

"Thought becomes action, experience, and memory. Dust is but an aid in creative thought.

"Thought, wonder, experience, love, none of these exist in the physical universe, and yet these are the only things you will bring with you to heaven one day.

"Fill your mind and heart as your adventure will be short.

"If you recognize my pattern, to create such an awesome physical universe from a single small form, consider the potential for the realm of heaven. Billions of souls bring to Me not one bit of dust, but instead their unique experience and intellect. Heaven is made from the astonishing intangible. I made the world such that souls could come back and decorate heaven. What awaits, you cannot comprehend. Go make your adventure without fear! Then, bring your paintbrush to heaven!"

Big Carp

Black Hawk Lake. To a boy, the name inspired images of Indian camps. Birch bark canoes, ready at a moment's notice for a dozen painted faces to jump in, grab paddles and streak across the water toward some purpose requiring immediate action.

"The salmon are running, jump in the canoes!"

"A woman is battling an alligator, quick! To the canoes!"

"A giant snake is eating all the fish! Into the canoes!"

Never mind that our canoes were old tire tubes, patched beyond their safe road limit, and put to use for summer camping trips. Endless imaginary scenarios required us to grab our tubes and run with wild abandon into the water.

The camping trip would begin on warm windy Friday mornings. Mom announced, "We're going camping this weekend, your dad will be home early!" Into action we sprang. We made piles of necessities in the middle of the bedroom floor. Things like BB guns, twine, pocket knives, hot wheels, hammers, and bed sheets. Bed sheets are useful survival tools for making bandages, hammocks, and ropes to rappel cliffs. But there was limited space, so Mom would remove most of the items and add useless stuff like underwear and socks. No one was ever saved from the wilderness by fresh underwear, so our weekend camp-outs included a degree of unnecessary risk caused by packing non-essentials.

The camper was parked at home in a walled off

section of the barn. Not willing to give up any space from the chickens, the compartment was two feet wider than the pop-up camper. Dad was a truck driver, and an expert at backing up trailers, so this worked out fine. But if he had gone to work on Friday, leaving the camper in the barn, Stevie and I were the only bodies skinny enough to squeeze our way in, open the little side door, and load our essentials.

After grilled cheese sandwiches and cartoons, we knew the hour was nigh. Dad would come home, change clothes, and off we'd go. We sat on the porch steps and waited. After hours of anxious waiting we would see him. A pickup truck being chased by a cloud of dust coming down the sun baked gravel road. As he pulled in the drive we would come running, ready to hug his legs and tell him we were going camping. Somehow, he always knew. "Go get ready or I'll leave you here!" While we had been ready for hours, we scattered to find critical forgotten items we required for a weekend in the wilderness.

The pickup eased up to the barn, the pop-up followed it out. The final packing was accomplished. With the girls up front, Stevie and I would jump in back of the pickup for the hour long drive. It wasn't bad. Dad had built a "topper" over the pickup bed, and the bedding for the trip would be tossed in back. Stevie and I lounged in the luxury of Sultans during our ride, while considering our options for when we arrived. Summer days are long, and the first night in camp still had time for swimming, camp fires, and spooky ghost games after dark.

Saturday would break with the smell of bacon mixed with lake water, trees, and mildew on canvas.

Saturday was about fishing. We never knew what the girls did on Saturday. Probably laundry or something not very interesting. Fishing had to be done on Saturday. The camp ground at Black Hawk Lake was next to a city park that wrapped around the north and west end of the lake. This was our normal fishing ground. As we fished, we looked across the lake to the far shore and on occasion, saw people fishing there. One day dad said, "Let's go ask the guy at the bait shop if the fishing is any good over there."

The bait shop was a walk across the park to the far side of the street, tucked between an alley and someone's garage. A grizzled old character with a two-day morning shadow would sit at a table and conduct business. He seemed to be missing a lot of parts. A handful of teeth on one side of his mouth were gone. One eye was droopy. There were fingers missing, and a leg that never seemed to move by itself. Dad asked him what the fishing was like on the other side of the lake. After a dramatic pause, the old man looked at Stevie and me with his bad eye and said, "I'm not sure I'd recommend the fishing over there. That's where the old blue cat took my leg and made me crippled!"

With complete indifference to the old man's condition, we launched into questions, and he reeled us in. "There's blue catfish in that lake, bigger 'en you boys. If you bring 'em in, they'll fight ya. They'll bite and shake their heads. They have daggers on their heads that'll kill a man who gets in the way. And they have poison whiskers they can wrap around your arm and leave burn marks and scars. You see these fingers?" He displayed his missing fingers, "If you catch an old blue cat and find them in his belly, bring them to me 'cause I want 'em back."

The tale sealed the deal. We were fishing for giant blue catfish on the other side of the lake. "What do we catch them with?"

"I have a secret recipe for my dough balls," and he proceeded to tell us his secret. "I mix corn meal and flour with black strap molasses. A little sugar and bacon fat makes 'em bite like crazy. But then again you might only catch little ones, only as long as my good leg." We bought the secret dough balls and Dad drove around the lake.

The groomed part of the park had ended, but we continued on to a gravel parking lot surrounded by knee high wilting grass trying to grow in sand. We hiked our gear to the shore and found a picnic table. Settled and ready, dough balls were applied and we commenced casting into Black Hawk Lake. The state limited us to two lines each in the water. We secured our first rod with rocks and sticks, watching with nervous anticipation for action while we prepared and cast our second line.

It was sunny, windy and hot, and we rolled up our jeans and waded into the water, holding our fishing poles, waiting for a giant blue cat to strike. And then, it happened! Stevie caught a fish! His rod bent over with the tip clear over in the water. He stood there holding on with both hands, afraid of being pulled in, and screaming for help. I watched, figuring any moment he would disappear and be pulled into the lake by a giant blue cat. These old cats doubtless, knew the fishing game well, and would pull in fishermen and eat them for lunch. It was us or them.

Dad ran over and held the rod while Stevie

reeled and reeled and reeled. He landed a nice carp. It was the biggest fish we had ever caught! It had almost killed Stevie! While Dad and Stevie were admiring the carp and putting it on a stringer, my pole jerked my arms. I screamed and pulled and backed my way out of the water. I pulled and reeled, and pulled and reeled. The sun passed overhead, Stevie and dad ate lunch, the milkman made rounds, a water ski team held their afternoon practice. It was taking a while to reel one in! My arms were aching and shaking, but after a time, another big carp was brought in. Rattled and shaking, landing on my knees, I looked at the rainbow shine across the fish scales. I saw the mouth gasping for air, the eye flicking back and forth. It was big and beautiful and I had won!

The morning continued, with frantic periods of carp battles, broken by interludes of quiet. It was the most perfect morning we had ever experienced. Dad was often busy helping with fish and lines and bait, so he had improvised a way to set up his fishing poles. He had pulled the picnic table down to the water's edge. With the reel on the ground, he positioned the rod up through the cracks between the boards that make the table top. With two poles secured, one set from either side of the picnic table, he figured he could safely fish without holding on to his poles.

His assumption was tested as the tip of one of his poles whipped itself over, slapping the table top, and pointing flat out toward the water. A fish at the other end took hold and wanted more than just the bait! Line screeched over the drag of the Zebco 404 that groaned in protest but held together. Dad went running for the pole, but then the picnic table slipped, was pulled, and turned sideways to the water! The rod tip bounced back once, the pole fell sideways out of its secure position between the table top boards, and fell. Without hitting the ground, the pole shot like an arrow following its line, across the shoreline and into the water. We stood, shocked, looking after it. After re-telling each other what we had just seen, we mused that it must have been one of the big blue cats. That fish had pulled a picnic table across the beach and taken the whole rod and reel! A story to remember and tell!

We held our lines knowing the giant hungry ones were now biting. Dad laughed, but he kind of missed his fishing pole and I felt sorry for him. But Dad was lucky, and not three minutes after losing his pole, he had another strike. It was a big one, he could tell. We had spooled up with twenty pound test line, never being too careful, and Dad was afraid he would break it. The drag on the reel whined, and Dad played the fish for the longest time. He found himself knee deep in the lake, and I worried if he slipped, he would follow his line into the lake just like his last fishing pole.

But then, he smiled and chuckled. He stopped reeling, bent over and laughed. After this bit of unexplained brevity, he got right back to business, tugging and reeling, and walked even further into the lake. Bending into the water he shouted, “Hey look at this!” Laughing again, he pulled up his other fishing pole! Somehow, as the big old fish had pulled in the rod it became entangled with Dad’s second line.

Dad was still standing at the water’s edge trying to dis-entangle the two poles when the line went tight.

Dad was wrapped up in two sets of fishing line with a big old fish pulling him in! “Ha! I’ve still got the fish!” Dad shouted. Hopelessly snarled, he threw the poles down, and began his fight with the fish in a hand-over-hand, inch by inch recovery of the line. Another big carp was landed, but this one with a camp fire story to be re-told for another fifty years. It was a perfect day.

Not everything was about fishing at Black Hawk Lake. There was a nice sandy beach, and the lake was shallow enough to warm up by July. If the wind died down in the evening, as it often did, the lake became glass smooth. By morning there would be fog and mist rolling about, rubbing it’s dampness into the grass, the sand, the tents, and the firewood.

After several trips to Black Hawk Lake we began to take our bicycles along. Our range of freedom tripled with bikes, and we ventured beyond the campground and the park. The town of Lake View nestled on one side, and we explored the quiet streets, the small-town grocer, and the gravel ally behind the grain elevator.

One quiet afternoon after a morning of fishing I decided to ride my bike around the lake. We could see the far shore and had often made the quick trip in the pickup truck. I might have taken a fishing pole, but decided my first trip was to just settle the details of getting there. While I didn’t know exactly how to get around the lake, if I kept the lake on my left I would make it all the way around. It started well enough.

A couple of left turns in town, and the lake was back on my left where it should be. I was on the road we took fishing for carp. Passing the familiar pull off to the rough beach areas, I entered unfamiliar territory. I was a long way from camp, but I knew my way back, and in the worst case, if roads didn't follow the lake, I could just reverse course.

Good solitary bike rides give way to scenery, fresh air, and time to daydream. With the wind at my back I made good progress to places I didn't know. The road kept to the lake and while the town was far behind, houses populated most of the shoreline. Comforting scenery but a sense of unfamiliarity to it. I had been keeping the lake on my left but paid little attention to it. Looking in detail, the lake had grown massive! It turned out the Black Hawk Lake at the campground was a little bay on a much, much larger lake. There were no familiar features around the shoreline, and somehow the far shoreline was now a long, long way across. I was almost lost.

Sometimes you get an odd feeling that you have two bad choices. The way back was known, but it was a long trip. The way forward was unknown, and it might extend just as far or farther. Or it might be just a little way. It was hot and windy and when I had started the wind was at my back. Now with wind crossing open water it was coming around to my face. I kept going.

The houses stretched forward along the shore, with farm fields on my right, and the road continued to circumnavigate the lake on my left. Nothing looked like a town or a campground. Turn around, hours of biking. Straight ahead, who knows? Each stroke of the peddles I would have to repeat for the trip back. The lake had beat me. I came over a small rise, with a blessed downhill slope that ramped into a little neighborhood. Downhill just meant going uphill on the way back. I stopped and began to turn the bike. Just then I saw people! Rescue! Soda pop! Well, let's not get excited. There was a woman at the road, looking in her mailbox. I rode up, stopped, and politely asked where the campground was.

She looked at me with an odd expression. I knew I was beat, wind-blown, and sun burned. But hey, everybody looked that way. Annoyed, she pointed, "It's right down there another block!" I rolled into the campground, embarrassed, relieved, and proud. Ready to go fishing!

Educational Opportunities

Mom had become a school teacher. The summers of market gardening were not keeping up with the growing demands of a bunch of kids. There was always that nagging worry of Dad falling over dead due to some strange catastrophe. Mom's greatest desire may have been to be a teacher, but it had to be explained. All ambitious folks with new careers take the love of their craft back home with them. For us, that meant we were to become the smartest children on earth. Games became educational. Puzzles more challenging. TV switched off earlier and more often.

The weekend outings to Black Hawk Lake changed. Mom decided that our Saturday afternoons of fishing, swimming, bike riding and climbing had to become more intellectual. Saturday afternoon excursions to places of historical or geographic interest were applied to the itinerary.

The process got off to a slow start. Cemeteries where dead people were buried. Old houses where people in the cemetery used to live. Statues of people who ended up in the cemetery. The fish were biting; I was sure. Mom highlighted the most educational parts of our tours. Dad seemed trapped in something he was sure would be worse if he attempted escape. A scandal, a crime, and a supernatural experience. Some combination of these is required to make a tourist destination successful. We didn't know it yet, but would soon discover this marketing secret in our venturing for great knowledge.

I rolled out early one Saturday to get in some fishing. Wet to my knees, mud over bare ankles, in the tall grass, Suzy managed to find me. “Hurry up, we gotta go see something.” We arrived at a hundred-year-old, white two story house. “Oh, boy! Here we go again.” Stevie and I lingered on the front porch as the donations were swapped for the brochure. The tour guide waited for a crowd of sufficient size to develop.

“Boys, this is a place of history,” the guide began, selling himself to the least interested members of the audience. “Not famous history, but a time capsule of sorts, preserved so we can step back in time and imagine life during the westward movement.” It wasn’t even famous. It was just an old house. Dad seemed able to close his eyes and sleep like a horse on his feet. “But there is a story attached to this house that has survived the ages and is responsible for its remarkable preservation. That work continues today with your kind and generous donations.” How did dad not fall over?

“This was a stage stop, along an old trail. We don’t know who started the trail. Perhaps the buffalo made the path, and the Indians followed it. The explorers, trail blazers, and guides came right down this very path, leading the wagons and gold miners and settlers. A stage route came through. At first the stages stopped and camped every night wherever darkness fell. Soon the best stops were set at regular intervals about a day’s ride apart. Entrepreneurs, or perhaps travelers tired of the trip, got off and built shelters, and then hotels for the travelers to use.

The railroad came down this path, and you can see the old depot just a few steps down the street. That railroad carries corn and coal now, but once brought the travelers west, right across our back yard here. Our story that lead to ruin and revival of this stage stop begins in that time.

There were four sisters running the stage stop. Their mama had died with their last baby sister in childbirth, leaving them as teenagers to run the operation. A few years later, their daddy was massacred by Indians while off running a herd with some cowboys." Stevie and I perked up. It seemed at least we were getting a good story. "The railroad made the stage stop a success, but the war between the states came along and was ruining their business. There were disagreements in the area over how northern or how southern one should be. Stages were robbed. Trains were diverted to the war effort. Travel through the area had slowed to a few adventuresome types, running to the promise of the west before the war caught up to them. A few deserters, too late to escape early, were betrayed by boots, buttons and equipment still hanging to their belts. The more notorious attracted bounty hunters. The hotel clientele had thinned out and roughened up."

"Now here we are standing in the parlor. A general gathering area, it has a long bar on this side, and the sisters were able to keep the place running by selling whiskey to the rough crowd. There were tables where you are standing, and gambling was encouraged. While the men spent hours wrestling money from each other, they built their courage, luck, and intuition with whiskey."

"That's not true," whispered Mom in our ears, "he's using oratory technique to keep us interested." It was definitely getting more interesting.

"On a hot summer night, just like today, the Picker brothers rode in. Four boys in another time, hardened as men by war, turned in to criminals by walking away. They acquired horses from a train that had slipped a track where a mysterious fire had burned out the ties. Moving west on trails far from the action, they arrived at our little stage stop. Dropping their reigns at the water tank, the four of them settled in for whiskey and cards. After time enough to hone their skills, they split up in pairs, and took on local boys heading east to join the war. Confident, or drunk the new recruits were on the road to glory. The whiskey, the heat, the hardened killers, the energy of recruits, words were said. Accusations made, and a gun appeared.

"Miss Nancy, the oldest of the four sisters was behind the bar. She reached beneath the counter and pulled her own gun, informing her guests to settle down. One of the Picker boys turned toward Miss Nancy with his gun drawn, and she fired, splitting his Adam's apple, leaving him to choke on his blood to die. Three more shots, and the Picker brothers were dead."

"It's unfortunate but history has its horrible moments," mom whispered, "We must learn from people's mistakes."

"Miss Nancy worried for her soul that night. As they buried the bodies in the grave yard, and yes folks you can walk right up the street here and find the four Picker brothers' graves in the cemetery behind the old Baptist church. Let's see where was I, Oh, yes, Miss Nancy sought guidance from the parson. New in town, the preacher was having difficulty building a following.

There was no church yet, making his task difficult. Assuaging her guilt, Miss Nancy offered her dining room at the stage stop for services on Sundays.

"And here in the dining room where we stand the tables pushed to the sides, the chairs were set as pews like a proper church. The stage didn't run Sunday, so whoever spent Saturday night was entitled to a good sermon. The preacher became famous for his spiritual awakening skills. Stories were told describing how he could grab your soul, take you to the edges of hell and roast the sin off the edges. You could feel the heat and would sweat 'til your clothes were drenched. When you were begging forgiveness, Jesus would appear. He would stand in the fires of hell for you and wash your soul with his cool refreshing tears as your unworthy soul left him standing there in the fiery furnace suffering for your sinful ways."

"Pay attention, boys!" Mom always relished a little fire and brimstone.

"Washed of their sins the patrons could resume their drinking and gambling with fresh vigor. Tables came back, cards dealt, chairs leaned back not quite tipping. It wasn't long after the Picker boys were shot that strange occurrences began." The guide's voice grew low. "Whiskey bottles would spill from the bar of their own volition. Cards would float from tables. Demons had taken up residence. On a hot summer Sunday, with the preacher in full throated oration, the Picker brothers' ghosts appeared as shimmering apparitions."

The ghosts spoke, "Just shut him up already. We can't take any more of that noise! Can we get him outta here!"

"Challenged by the evil apparitions the preacher launched into his finest stew of exorcism and deliverance. Chairs flew, glass broke, candles melted, and draperies burst into flame. Week after week on Sundays at the stage stop great battles between good and evil were fought. For a while the great commotions drew a crowd from the area. Better than vaudeville, the script was different every week. Sometimes the preacher and congregation fled the scene. On other occasions the Picker brothers wailed off into the ether.

"Rumors spread, and the antics of the Picker brother's ghosts warded off the regular business. Pragmatic and absolved on a weekly basis, the four sisters decided to offer additional services at a price for the pleasure of men. Financial disaster was averted once again, and the annoyances of the Picker brothers were mere distractions from the colorful attire the sisters now sported. Right up these stairs we can see the rooms the four sisters were using."

"You boys might want to go outside now and see the garden." But we were embracing the educational excursion.

"Mom the guide said 'apparition'. We're learning new vocabulary!" Mom had that concerned look on her face, but that was normal. Dad looked like he was caught being interested in unauthorized scripture. We shuffled up the steps with the crowd.

"It seemed the Picker brothers were losing their battle with the preacher, and the four sisters were recovering their business reputation. Now standing here in this room we can imagine the scene that played out the night it reached a climax. Nellie, the second sister, had beguiled the local senator into this very room, and they had gotten down to business on this very bed. It was at that moment when one of the Picker brothers came right through that mirror above the bed and started flying around the chandelier. The Senator screamed, jumped to his feet, and ran out the door. What do you think son, can you imagine a ghost coming through that mirror right at you? Scare you some, wouldn't it?"

As I was still imagining the getting down to business part, the scary stuff hadn't occurred to me yet. The guide continued with the suggestiveness of an R-rated movie with the pictures removed for family viewing.

"The Senator ran ~~naked~~ right over the balcony railing and spilled himself on to a poker game below. Nancy came running ~~naked~~ behind him but stopped short of the rail. While the table broke his fall, the Senator had exposed a player's hand holding four aces. Hands grabbed the pot, and a gun fired. 'It was her fault!' as the politician passed the blame. A shot rang out from the bar below, and the entire place erupted in gun fire. If you look around, you can still find the bullet holes in the walls. This time the four sisters fell. Right there at your feet is where Nellie landed. You can lift your shoe and still see a blood stain." I looked down and imagined a naked Nellie.

"The property fell to disrepair for years. A young man inherited the property and came back wounded from World War 1. He lived here until he went crazy. No one knows his full story and his ghost isn't sayin'. But he is found sobbing on September nights in the garden. They pulled his bones out of here one day, and yes you can find his grave down the street as well.

"A destitute young soldier's widow moved in during World War II. No one minded, and she stayed. The county eventually granted her title. She began the women of fallen soldier's organization and started restoration. Your generous donations help keep our stage stop and its unique history alive. Hope you enjoyed the tour folks!"

Stevie and I compared notes as we road in the back of the truck to the camp ground. Mom and Dad were finishing some kind of argument as we unloaded and made a bee line for our bikes.

The next week Suzy found us again and hauled us with a little less reluctance in for our next educational adventure. Dad announced he had learned of a cave in the region. There was nothing like a nice cool cave tour on a hot summer afternoon. Mom seemed satisfied moving our lessons from history toward geology.

Down a wooded path and across a hay field we opened a lonely gate as we came to the cave. It seems caves cannot locate themselves next to convenience stores and highways. They are where they are. At the cave the common routine of changing money for brochures and a tour guide commenced. We donned kerchiefs and baseball hats because it rained little waterfalls in the cave.

The education began. "This here cave was discovered by a farmer's cow back in the early nineteen hundreds. The cow fell in right there where we climbed down and bellered away until someone found her." The tour guide slipped into the textbook lexicon of rocks, minerals, and formations. Somehow glaciers ground the dinosaurs into buffalo and squeezed water into the ground and left dirt all over. It wasn't our first cave tour, and the mind wanders. "Now in this large open cavern we can see where old Dinky Herber started his business runnin' moonshine."

Mom shot a look at Dad, who returned a, "What did I do?" look back at her. Stevie and I perked up.

"The operation stands here today just as she was left in 1925. Old Dinky wasn't sharing in the prosperity of the roarin' twenties like most folks and needed an edge. With the discovery of this cave, and surrounded by barley, wheat, rye, and corn an idea formed. God's pure water running right through this cave was mixed with grain and roasted to mash. If you look back along this wall of the cave, you can see where the smoke from the fires would rise and disappear into that crack. That crack goes to the surface, so old Dinky could fire up his mash and stills down here in peace and comfort. You can imagine how good it must have smelled, roasting grain with a wood fire. Just like Grandma's kitchen cookin' bread. Any questions?"

My hand shot up just ahead of Mom's eyes to keep them down. "Yessir young man what's on yer mind?"

"How do you make whiskey?" the blaze from Mom's eyes raised the illumination within the cave.

"Well, shucks that's a good question." Our tour guide seemed to have the sure kind of knowledge that comes from deep personal experience. Grain was mixed with water and cooked and dried and ground and cooked some more. It sat in barrels for a while, and then it was boiled in the still. The whiskey formed as the liquid parts evaporated and then re-liquefied while the solid stuff just became cattle feed. We joked about happy cows. This, our first chemistry teacher, wore a scraggly grey beard, a red bandana over a tan bald spot, and was missing a few teeth.

Stevie continued with the questions, “why did he make whiskey?”

“Well, there’s another good question, and it leads to my next part of the tour. You see whiskey was in great demand because it was illegal. Things that are illegal seem to draw good money.”

“You boys shouldn’t listen to this!” came a hiss from behind us.

“For a while ol Dinky was happy just makin’ and sellin’ whiskey. But after a’piece, he started having a few parties in here. Mostly card games with fellas he was doin business with. As we get a little deeper in the cave here, you can see a nice wide flat spot. Right here people started comin’ round to play their saxophones and horns. This attracted the women too. My mama used to say sin and crime share the same cell, and it wasn’t long before old Dinky lost control of his place. Besides ramping up whiskey production, depravities of the underworld crept in and found a home.”

“Why did people like whiskey?” Stevie was still at it. Mom hadn’t stood on his foot like mine.

“It’s been said Dinky’s whiskey had a strange effect on people. It felt like it was burning your throat on the way down, but when it hit your stomach all your problems in the world went away. If you woke up the next day, you wouldn’t remember a thing. So, people came and partied and forgot they were even here. Somehow, they kept stumbling back to rediscover the place, and demand for production kept rising. Dinky became rich, and local townspeople talked and wondered how a farmer dressed so well.

"Dinky's secret recipe that made you forget kept his operation safe for years. But one night a righteous woman was shamed, a sheriff was bribed, a politician threatened, and a gangster was shot along with an innocent bystander. Everyone left and cleaned up, but the funerals demanded stories. Holes in the stories created rumors, and the rumors became tips to federal agents. On a summer morning, just like this, federal agents followed Dinky and his crew to his cave. The agents entering the cave met bullets and buckshot and retreated. Not having the manpower or firepower to go in, they pulled their truck up to the cave. Tying a rope to a boulder they dragged it across the entrance, sealing in Dinky and six of his boys.

"Smoke was seen from the vent hole for fourteen days after that. And then it went cold. Agents sat by the boulder for a month and left. Nobody went back in, and as time passed the whole affair slipped into legend. The current owner heard the legend while having breakfast at the Highway café, right there in town. He came out, moved the boulder, and found seven perfectly preserved bodies lying in the cave. He said they looked like they were still sleeping after a solid night of drinking.

"That very night ghosts danced amongst the trees in the orchard at the mouth of the cave. They've never bothered anyone. When the moon sits just right, you can see them rambling between the trees, having a good party. For an extra ticket, we host ghost spotting parties on Friday nights all summer.

"We have a special treat for you. In the deepest room of the cave you can see here seven pine boxes where the remains of Dinky and his boys are. The boxes are suffering some from water and mold, so I suppose the boys will spill out of their boxes in another few years. It'll be interestin' to see how preserved they still are.

"Thanks for the tour folks. Don't forget when you get to the parkin' lot to stop by the gift shop and whiskey bar!"

We finished that summer visiting cemeteries and statues. As August waned and that terrible night before the first day of school arrived, mom gathered us around to ask what we had learned that summer. The girls learned about weaving cloth from flax and who built the cemetery. Stevie said he learned how to make whiskey. I learned about a bar fight with naked women and ghosts.

It seems after people get used to their jobs for a while, they get less excited about them. We didn't have to be the smartest kids in the class anymore. We didn't have to take educational excursions during our camp-outs. It's better to keep work separate from the family.

Lead My Sheep

An annual event in the late summer draws the county residents together. Farmers, craftsmen, cooks, and gardeners bring their best together for a great gathering. And while the judges are looking over the finest of sweet corn and embroidery, the neighbors engage in other grand contests. Horses are raced, husbands are yelled for, and dogs obey. Bright ribbons in blue, red, and white are awarded, and the proud contestants beam. We peek at sideshow oddities and a carnival erupts as the sun goes down. It is the county fair.

Mom and Dad had work to do and would show up on the days that mattered most. But someone in the neighborhood was always spending the day at the fair. With a few phone calls mom would be free of us boys for most of a week in August. “Be sure to thank them for the ride and here give them a pie.” I think the pie insured our ride home. I could imagine one of the neighbors late in the evening ready to head home finding their car, “Hey, look at that pie in the front seat. Oh, yeah, we have to take Darlene’s boys back home!”

Arriving before the main events started, Stevie and I would set out to find school friends long lost since June. I would find my best friend Kenny tending to his show calf. He always had a show calf and by August it was in beautiful shape. Kenny explained the technical side of being a cattleman, “The judges want to see a nice straight back across here. And he has to weigh in pretty high but not too high. I have an angus so he needs a nice shiny coat. He has to follow me when I lead him." This year was Kenny's sixth entry, and he was aiming for grand champion. He would stay busy until they showed the cattle, so I wandered around to the sheep.

My friend Brad was showing sheep this year. He had finished as a pathetic and tragic herdsman three years in a row. I met him at the pen. "What's up Brad?"

"Hey, I'm glad to see you. I need someone to help show lambs. I must show them all at once and I have no one to help. Can you and Stevie help out? It's easy!"

Once again Brad seemed in desperate need on his way to catastrophe. "What do we do?" A quick lesson in leading the sheep delivered, we each selected a lamb for practice. They loved to be lead, so that was no problem. We reviewed technique for settling beside them and holding them in position for judging. The trickiest part was to get down on one knee next to the sheep wrap one arm over the back and hold them on the belly while the other arm held the jaw up nice and straight. The lambs were docile and cooperative. If you were genuine and firm they went along with it. It seemed easy enough.

Lesson delivered, Brad was engrossed in scrubbing and brushing his lambs. "What are you doing?"

"I'm whitening the lambs. Every year I get marks for not looking clean enough. But they are washed and combed the best I can. So this year I'm applying a little special detergent. 'Smashing Bright Miracle Wash'."

"Hey, I've seen that advertised on TV. Don't they

use that for dishes and laundry and car washes?"

"Yup, and I will have the whitest sheep out there today." To the credit of the Smashing Bright company the sheep were turning a dazzling bright white. One could say they glowed under the lights. A step above the lambs in other pens, we were excited because Brad could win, rookie handlers and all.

The hour came, and we followed the parade of handlers and sheep into the judging arena. A smattering of viewers was in the stands including a gaggle of girls from West County high school. Every year Kenny and Brad and I would stumble in to these same girls at the fair, basketball games, and track meets. Compared to regular girls at our high school these were exotic girls from a different town. Much more exciting. My pulse jumped a notch as we lined up, hit a knee, and nestled up to our lambs. I didn't look up at them. My sheep and I froze, a set of glowing porcelain statues, waiting for the minute to pass when we could move again.

The judges made their way down the row. While sheep were judged as a "pen" they were given individual examinations. My lamb was perfect. She rested her jaw in my hand and viewed the judges without interest. A real pro. The judges entered our direct field of view, walked around us, made a few comments and notes, and moved along. I relaxed just a bit and felt something funny in my hand under the belly. Worried, I moved my hand, and it seemed the lamb's nice stiff gleaming white coat was moving with my hand. Gentle as a mother with a sleeping baby I made a discreet move and glanced down at my arm. As it moved, the lamb's wool coat stuck to my arm. It lifted right off the back. I could see the pink flesh as if I was peeling back a wrapper.

What was I going to do? When it was time to go, my lamb would drop half its coat! I glanced at Brad to my left. He was watching the judges not noticing that as his arm moved a pink line of flesh was showing on his lamb too!

Sometimes in life there is nothing to do but proceed into the maw of the monster. I waited, motionless, planning to turn my sheep away from the crowd as quickly as possible. The judges walked past in reverse order, making momentary glances, raising fresh sweat on my brow. A signal was given, and we rose and paraded out in line. The judges were walking off, the crowd was standing and planning their next event to attend. Stevie got lucky, leading a normal looking lamb ahead of us. Brad's pen looked good until I stood up. A four-inch wide swath of wool that had rested under my arm fell as an unbroken strip to the arena floor. A glowing white turd on a golden straw mat. I glanced away from the crowd and back toward Brad. With a shocked expression, he was looking at a strip of wool sticking to his arm.

Follow the procession, don't look up, don't look to the side. Between the teeth, into the gullet, the monster will consume you fast enough. It took ten steps before someone laughed. Maybe fifty more steps. By the time we were out of sight I could hear the girls from West County screaming my name and laughing.

We got to the pen and sat around to consider the disaster. I tried to cheer Brad up, "Well you can't finish worse than last year!" The sheep were dropping their coats like feeding bread to pigeons. Brad kept busy raking up wool and depositing it to the manure pile at the end of the barn. In fifteen minutes Brad had a pen with bare pink sheep.

Visitors were walking past with embarrassed smiles as their children would point and say, “Look daddy, what kind of animal is that? Hey look at the giant rats! Whatever happened to those poor beasts!” Adults made comments as if they were private but loud enough to be heard. The kids just shouted what they thought. Brad was suffering.

Not long after reaching full nakedness, the judges arrived to award the ribbons to each pen. Three judges, approached and stumbled to a stop with shocked looks. “Where are your sheep?”

“This is them.” Brad took on an air of complete nonchalance. “How’d we do?”

“But these are not the sheep we judged. They had beautiful white coats. I distinctly remember them!”

“Yup, but it must be over a hundred degrees in here. I wasn’t letting ‘em suffer one minute longer so, I sheared ‘em.” The judges turned in upon themselves and began a harmony of furious whispers.

“We’ll be made fools! Everyone will think it’s a joke! How can we disqualify? But the presentation is over!” And on it went. Brad remained as cool as the head on a mug of root beer. A sheep barn is a peaceful place. The gentle baa’ing of the animals, the delightful giggles of children, the smiles and cooing of adults around lambs. The little erupting volcano of judges had moved off to the center of the aisle where they could whisper louder. Brad sat on a bale, chewing the fibrous end of a wheat straw.

Yes, sometimes in life there is nothing to do but

proceed to the maw of the monster. The judges turned with fallen faces and walked toward Brad. “We wish to congratulate you with this year’s grand champion ribbon.” Delivered with as little enthusiasm possible, tight smiles, and weak handshakes they exited the scene before the ribbon was posted over the pen. Brad was ecstatic and so were we!

The story spread across the fairground and soon everyone was making their way to see the pink grand champion lambs. Smashing Bright Miracle Wash remained a secret.

Dad's Tractor

The folks didn't go to the fair every day. Mom would come on 4-H days when the girls were showing canned pickles and pies. Dad might make it for an evening or two. The one sure day dad spent at the fair was tractor pull day. Dad had driven trucks and tractors throughout their early development and loved to see every class of the event.

The tractor pull would start with the non-professional lighter classes and move up in size and weight with winners and losers apparent for everyone to see.

Professionals pulling with heavy versions of iconic brands kept the evening going strong. When they were done, the super modified classes came along to highlight the show. Tractors with two engines, special fuels, giant tires, polished and dressed for battle. By the time the super-modified's began it would be dark. Their roll cages bejeweled in lights and blinkers demanded rapt attention. Their engines pouted and complained as they paraded up to the sled. Once hooked and ready the silver suited driver would turn his moonwalker's helmet and give a "thumbs up." Thc dragon's bclly would rumble then roar. Fire would push flumes of white smoke from the exhaust pipes. We covered our ears. Popping the clutch the tires put the beast in motion throwing damp earth in the air, groaning under the weight of the sled but determined to move the load forward. Settling to a deep growl that would reverb on our chests, we had perhaps a dozen seconds to witness the struggle.

The crowd would shout and holler in comic silence, their shouts overwhelmed by the noise from the track. Snippets of the announcer's voice over the loudspeakers were heard, "One sixty... one seventy... he's going to... two hun... he's about...." The sled's giant weight crept toward the hitch assured of eventual victory over the beast. By now the tractor's front wheels were in the air. The silver man throttled with precision to keep the tractor pulling, but not flipping. Tires spun, smoke blew. Feet, then inches, were gained until the sled stopped moving. At that point the track judge brandished the red flag. Wounded in its charge, the beast settled to a puffing smoking remnant.

Dad would turn to us, smiling and laughing, and then give us his analysis. "He let his wheels get up too early. There's no momentum, only torque. You're better off getting distance while the wheels can grip the track, then let her go once the engine pulls down far enough..." Dad was in his one and only fantasy.

A year came when the fair had a "working man's" class for the tractor pull. Tractors were to have no modifications other than front wheel weights. The tractor had to show up ready to work on the farm. For safety, the red flag would fall when the skid stopped, or if the front tires came off the track, even once. A friendly competition amongst neighbors. Dad was in. The only problem was our tractor.

Utilitarian. About as kind as words come to describe dad's tractor. There was nothing sexy about dad's tractor. Stolen once only to be returned by the thief. One bright winter morning we awoke to dad rushing in the house to call the sheriff. The tractor was normally parked in an open lean-to next to the garage. That morning, it was missing. The sheriff came out and followed tracks across the drive and up the road. But the traffic and hard-packed gravel gave up its clues after the first mile. The sheriff put out the word, with difficulty. “She’s an old Case, but you can’t tell because the markings are all gone. There’s a home-made front end loader on her. Just a big rusty squared off thing. Chains on the tires. No cab. Sort of cream and grey but covered in dirt.”

A hopeless description of something no one would ever notice. But four days later the tractor showed up back in its spot. Calling the Sheriff again, they speculated. “Must have had second thoughts.”

“Looks like he washed it.”

“Probably thinking to paint it up and sell it.”

“Hard to sell this one. Those custom running boards let me stand on it to pick fruit. Kind of easy to mix up the wheel clutches too. Gotta let them go just right or you can tip her. Can’t see over the front- end loader but I made it big enough to clear the cattle stalls in one trip. Lights and gauges don’t work. Wonder how he even got it home.”

Dad called the fair board to make sure his customizations didn’t disqualify his tractor. He entered the tractor in the ultra-lightweight class and started practicing. Piles of fence posts were pulled. Tree stumps were yanked from the ground. An ancient old wreck was pulled out of a muddy hole. Work was accomplished that had been waiting years for a better day.

The working man’s class began early in the day. Neighbors were chuckling over their equipment, openly wondering if they were made of the right stuff. But dad was a resolute competitor. Fussing over his tractor, he skipped the opportunity to review the field. He had placed a tarp over the massive home- built bucket on the front-end loader. The track judge approached each tractor and discussed rules with its operator. When he got to dad, he wanted to see what was under the tarp. Dad lifted it for the judge to view, and a discussion resulted. The judge relented and laughed, saying, “well it’s the working man’s class I guess.”

The rules allowed for weight to be added to the front of the tractor to keep the wheels down while pulling. Weights were considered standard equipment for farmers, and most often comprised of heavy iron plates stacked on a rack near the front axle. While dad didn’t have fancy wheel weights, he read the rules liberally and figured he could add weight using the massive loader bucket to its advantage. But what to use that would pass muster with the judge?

The competition proceeded from the lightest to heaviest tractor within each class. There were two tractors ahead of dad. The first guy blew it. He revved his engine, popped the clutch, and immediately bounced his front tires up. The track judge reminded everyone that wheels up was fine for the professionals, but for safety in this class that was the end of the run. The second farmer was a neighbor with a nice looking Ford. He got started and gradually kept moving the throttle with progress down the track. A respectable forty feet later, his front wheels lifted finishing his run.

Dad wheeled the old tractor up to the skid. Dirty, ugly, and old. “Don’t break her Merle!” yelled someone from the crowd. Dad waved. He jumped down and pulled the tarp off the front of the tractor. The home-made front end loader appeared as an enormous cancerous tumor. Out of proportion and wearing its patina of rubbed rust, the worst came next. Dad had loaded the bucket full of manure. Flies and all, a glorious rotting pile was the predominate feature displayed for all the fair to see. After a collective gasp, the crowd laughed. “Don’t spill any Merle!” Dad waved again, and the crowd buzzed that maybe Merle was smart after all. We cringed in our seats, and then we moved to the top row hoping to avoid recognition and embarrassment.

Dad gave his thumbs up just like a pro and smoothly moved the throttle lever down. His arms flew as he adjusted clutches, brakes, and throttle. The old tractor moved, preoccupied with her load of manure, not noticing the weight on her tail. Dad stayed in motion, disciplined and focused. He didn’t look back at the skid. He didn’t look at the crowd. The engine would bog, and the throttle would move. A little left, and a clutch lever moved.

Despite the flurry at the controls, the old tractor went about her chores with determination. The four cylinders whined for fuel and growled a bit more. Plodding, balancing a huge load of manure, she struggled forward. And forward and forward. The crowd cheered. “Keep her goin’ Merle!” And with a deft hand, dad kept her going forward, inch by inch, never stopping. All the years spent studying the professionals from the grand stand was paying off. The skid always wins, but dad made ninety feet, and won his class that day. He was as happy as any super-modified champion.

Dad took time-off and spent the week at the fair that year. Neighbors talked for years, and the tractor was fixed and kept in use beyond a practical life. The ultra-lightweight tractor pull champion of Sioux county.

Pie

The county fair has something for everyone. Even the girls enjoyed the fair. Domestic 4-H projects occupied three large metal frame buildings. Most folks would walk through to escape the August heat and pour over the stitch work, the table settings, fresh picked flower arrangements, and canned produce. 4-H gardens reared edibles that looked too good to eat, too large for one sitting, and polished to sparkle more than the dinnerware.

Then there were pies. Mom was an expert at deserts, and pies were the ultimate test of a desert chef. Mom's true homemade lemon meringue, stiff enough to hold up to a summer day was still a local legend. This year Suzy was entering an apple pie. We ate pie every night for a month to prepare for the fair. A perfect home-made crust, in a perfect new steel pan. A cross braided top crust, each individual strip of crust ending at a flute on the side of the pie pan. Tightly woven with just a hint of filling bubbling at each crossing layer of crust, dusted with white and brown sugar to sparkle and glow. The pie was joined with a crisp recipe card and set upon a home-embroidered dish cloth. Pastoral Americana set upon a table to evoke memories and senses.

Big sis won. With the world's best desert coach, it was predestined. While the judging is done in the 4-H buildings, the pies were part of a special event that married the elite of the domestic categories with the elite of the barn yard.

Iowa has more hogs than people and sporting its

place as the leading hog producer in the nation with pride. But Sioux County was more than hogs. Sioux County claimed to be the largest beef producing county in the nation. With the world's largest stock yards, and a dozen packing plants in Sioux City, the claim may well have been true. Beef was special. The grand champion steer at the fair would draw a crowd that would make Moses nervous about golden calves again.

The custom was to auction the grand champion beef and the runners-up at the show barn. Famous regional restaurants fought for the right to serve these steaks to customers for premium prices. Grand champion beef brought several multiples of market prices, and farmers would smile and shake their heads and think about next year. Then, for desert, the custom was to auction the top pies to the same crowd. The show barn filled to the brim. The grand champion steer had sold for a record price, and in the afterglow the crowd was happy and content to enjoy the pie auction. This year, big sis would stand right where the grand champion steer had stood, while the auctioneer took bids from the crowd for her pie. Everyone in Sioux County would watch.

Tradition creates not just memories, but conversation and anticipation for the next time. In the normal practice, every bidder who won a pie would step forward, collect his pie, and get to kiss the cook. Embarrassed pecks on the cheeks between neighbors added a dose of sex appeal to the show. The blue-ribbon pies had brought forty to fifty dollars apiece. Big sis came forward with her grand champion apple pie. The bidding crossed fifty, then seventy, then a hundred dollars in quick succession! Something had happened for the pie bidding. The crowd searched for the two remaining bidders to sort out the grudge match. The air in the auction barn was charged with electricity.

On one side was Doyle Hamm, the largest cattle farmer in Sioux County. A force to be reckoned with, his boy had produced the grand champion steer and it looked like he wanted the grand champion pie to celebrate. On the other side was Gus Neal. Gus made a fortune playing the risky game of brokering in cattle at the stock yards. A battle of local titans had begun, and the whole county picked sides and cheered them on.

The bidding became more deliberate. “Come on Doyle, this is the best pie in the county. You know her mother’s reputation for pie.” Mom blushed at dad, and he laughed and squeezed her.

“She’s gonna do all right I think!” dad replied.

“Don’t let this one get away Gus!” the auctioneer kept the bidders in the auction with help from the crowd. A hundred fifty. A hundred seventy-five. A record setting pie would be news in the Sioux City Journal!

“Two hundred fifty!” and Doyle was still having fun after his son’s success.

“Sold! For two hundred fifty dollars!” The crowd went wild. Given a moment for the crowd to settle, it was time to watch Doyle come out of the crowd, collect his pie, and kiss my sister. The crowd turned to Doyle, but Doyle turned to his sons beside him.

“Better go collect it boys,” and he looked down the bleachers at his seven sons. They all stood up, and stepped forward, forming a line, youngest to oldest. The crowd figured out what was happening and signaled their approval. The youngest stepped up for his kiss, followed by the next brother, and the next, until they all got to kiss the pie queen. A crescendo of applause came with each brother until the oldest gave his kiss and collected the pie.

In a normal year, the Sioux City Journal ran a front page photo and article of the grand champion steer for Sioux county. While the lead article appeared just as expected, the photo just below the headline was not a steer draped in a ribbon. That year it was a photo of the Doyle boys lined up and big sis holding her pie.

Clues

The little soul arrived at the edge of heaven and was gazing at its beauty in the distance. He could feel the music. He could sense the love. Another soul appeared. "Are you sleeping too?" he inquired. Other souls appeared, and they were sleeping too. For a moment, as they arrived, each would bask in the nearness of heaven. Exchanges amongst the souls began. Excited and earnest, they had stories and concerns about their ongoing personal journeys.

The little soul pressed a question, "How am I to complete my purpose if I know nothing of God while I'm awake?"

A soul named Cassie spoke up, "If people had absolute knowledge of heaven, they wouldn't work at their purpose. They'd quit their lives and wait to come back home. But God has a plan for us, and we must work at it. Did He explain fear and faith yet?"

Another soul named Nuriel spoke up, "You know God's love. You must feel it when you are awake."

"But I don't. I don't know He's there when I'm awake. I never seem directed toward my purpose. I seem to be focused on everything else. I can't hear Him."

"Little soul," Jas began. Jas spoke with the cadence of many years. "We have been where you are. You are a young person, meant to experience life. The great thoughts will come to you. Look for clues. If you get good at discovering God's clues, your faith and understanding will grow!"

"What clues!" And the small group of souls were

bursting to offer their help. Ideas flew in rapid succession.

"I find clues in music! When the music is playing, my soul is connected to my mind. That's when I can find my direction."

Cassie continued the thought, "There have been people in history given spiritual experiences, or fantastic gifts. Some of these are written or recorded. Some are embedded in art. I can find the clues when I am reading, and my soul and mind come together."

"I find clues in nature," another soul had joined the group, "The fascinating detail of God's smallest creatures. The coordinated beauty of natural cycles. The sky and the weather. It's easy to connect with my mind when God's work is sitting right before my eyes. The clues are there to see!"

Nuriel started another thought, "I find clues when I'm working hard. I get focused with a group of people, and suddenly my hands and mind are moving but I'm no longer directing them."

The group continued, "Oh, yes! Clues are in people! Many create and work in ways that can only come from God. Some are great speakers. Others are great problem solvers. Some care for others. Watch for people who are great at what they do. Look for people that enjoy their work."

Jas interrupted, "Little soul, when you are awake you must work on faith. Look for the clues. With every clue, you find faith. Ask God for help, but make sure you are looking, and listening. You must do your part. Your soul will find them, your mind will know when it happens!"

Sixteen

I gazed upon her, sitting in the shade under an apple tree. She was beautiful. All the right curves in all the right places. I had heard she was fast. I heard she had some history with an older man. But a young man full of desire overlooks such things. I was sixteen and ready. Determined to make her mine, the time for the impertinent question arose. “How much?”

“Two hundred fifty.”

“That’s a sad looking rear end,” I feinted.

“That’s all the style these days.”

“A lot of mileage, maybe she’s wore out.”

“Just needs a brake job, but you can do that yourself. Ha! She’s always been pretty fast without brakes, though!”

Perhaps it was the wad of money gripped in my hand with my driver’s license still warm from the laminator at the department of motor vehicles. Perhaps my desire was too obvious. Perhaps I was sitting in the driver’s seat refusing to budge. We settled at two hundred fifty.

First cars come at an impressionable age. Freedom, responsibility, freedom, maintenance, freedom, gas money. It was all about freedom. Every sixteen-year-old boy had the same purpose for owning a car. It meant no more school bus!

Using the school bus as a form of rural public transportation had grown stale. It went to the same places every day. The passengers were the same. If you wanted to date a girl, your choices were constrained to the girls on your route. Even worse, I seemed to be the choice for every girl on our route who couldn't get a date elsewhere. But now every place in the world, and every girl in the world seemed available.

I turned the key and put her in gear. The old shyster I made the deal with lived three hills and around two bends from home. The country roads were gravel and uncrowded. I was taking her home regardless of conditions. Starting down the first hill, I discovered the brake pedal would reach the floor without resistance. Improvising, I learned to navigate between the hard-packed tracks on the road using the loose gravel on the sides as friction for braking. Not too bad. A quick turn at the top of the hill and down we went into the deep valley. It was straight until the bottom, no worries yet. The accelerator was working just fine. I rolled the window down and felt the breeze. Alone as a driver, no parent or instructor. Just me and my car!

"G" forces are interesting. At rest a body feels the effect of one unit of gravity. But under acceleration a body will experience its inertia resisting such rapid changes. Measured in "G" force units every additional "G" feels like another body weight. It pushes you through the seat and flattens your face. Bugs splat on the windshield, experiencing rapid deceleration into a hard object. Vision tunnels forward. The "G" force has an upside I discovered, as it tended to limit how hard I was pushing on the gas pedal. One should let up while going downhill.

Some variety of animals appeared in the road toward the bottom of the hill. Screaming and steering were sufficient to avoid direct hits. At such a speed, it was hard to know what kind of animals they were, but they seemed to be riding bicycles. I guess shock waves caused by objects traveling at supersonic speeds can be destructive.

Any good stock car racer will tell you the corners are the most exciting. It is true. After thousands of cars worked the bend at the bottom of the hill, the loose gravel migrated to the outside of the corner. Years of working gravel over the outer edge caused the ditch to disappear. The road sloped upward into a fence row made of trees with barbed wired tacked between them. A hard packed clay track with a slight bank formed the inside of the corner. Good drivers from both directions stayed on the hard packed inside track. But I was not yet a good driver, and I was convinced that loose gravel was an effective braking system.

Another thing I learned about "G" forces. If one makes a turn on an embankment, the inertial forces push you into the seat. However, if one makes the turn on the loose gravel at the top edge of the bend the "G" force presses you sideways across the front seat. Weeks later I noticed the trees along the bend in the road had died. Upon closer inspection, their trunks were full of embedded gravel. Holes had punctured clean through in dozens of places. Tire tread marks seemed to trace just above the root line. The mysteries of science.

Coasting to the top of the hill at home, I rolled her over my bicycle to bring her to a stop. A transition had been made. The first order of business was to wash and wax her. The brake job followed. Of course learning begins by tearing things apart. Working the jack and removing the wheel was familiar territory. On a farm flat tires are a daily occurrence. I pulled the wheel off and rolled it toward the back of the car to Steve. “Here, grab this,” as I gave it a spin in his direction. He turned it mid-roll, and it wobbled toward the ground. “What do you think this is?” And disassembly began.

Some hours later it was time to try out the brake job. “Where’d you put the tire?”

“I set it right there behind the car.” Except it was nowhere to be seen. It’s always disconcerting when an inanimate object disappears. There was no doubt a tire came off the car. I had seen Steve tip it down behind the car. We looked in ever wider circles. Steve and I looked at each other with dread as realization touched us. The tire had not flopped down, but had somehow kept rolling. We lived on a hill. We walked to the edge, and looked down to see the tire, floating in the lake, as if taking a nice summer’s day swim.

“I wish I had seen it.”

“Yeah, me too. Look at the track through the grass.”

“Right over the little ski jump too.”

“God, I bet it was beautiful. Went through the fence too. Didn’t stop.”

“I’ll bet it was fast.” We looked at each other for a moment, and without a word reluctantly decided to not repeat the tire roll. After swimming fifty yards to retrieve it, fishing it out, and making the long roll back up the hill, we were sure that experiment was done. As I woke up from a nap, I noticed Steve looked tired as he finished cresting the hill with the tire.

The road we knew on a bicycle took on new characteristics. With traffic, the road had three hard packed tracks. The center track was where people put their left wheels. The two outside tracks were where they would put their right wheels. If you ever met someone while driving on the road, a game of chicken ensued. Both oncoming cars would want to maintain control of their left wheels on the center track. But of course, there was only one center track. Whoever moved off to their right would be sucked in to the loose gravel. The road would grab the steering wheel and control of the car. With practice, a good driver could anticipate which direction the car would fishtail in the loose gravel. He would spin the wheel back and forth in opposite directions to counter the natural amplification of a swinging mass. The car would oscillate between the attracting forces of an oncoming car to the left, and the ditch to the right. It never occurred to us that slowing down might also work.

A cool cat, could pull off the maneuver with practice. There was a pattern to follow. With an approaching car, increase your speed to heighten your trailing dust plume, and maintain your center lane dominance. Similar to peacocks starting a fight, the bigger plume wins. Just when it looks like the other driver will relent, enter the gravel surf with sharp quick motions. With the timing just right, you swing your front tires at the oncoming car with the closing distance about a car length apart. This action counters the first fishtail taking your front end into the ditch, and your rear coming around into traffic. But there are better reasons. Showing your tire treads to oncoming traffic at high speed and close proximity ensures the victory. Time slows down, the other driver's pupils dilate, their face is drawn in surprise and fear. If you can manage, give a wry smile and offer a nonchalant one handed wave, while using the other to whip the wheel back. Avoiding collision, cut across the oncoming traffic's tail and disappear in a dust cloud to the center lane dominant position. Having demonstrated cool graciousness your victory is complete. It can raise the pulse a bit.

I learned that cars eat money. Money comes from working. People work in order to drive cars. But the payoff was freedom. The horizon moved as we drove to it. The people we played with and worked with expanded as we explored the county line roads. Our ideas grew. Our world grew. New limits to a new horizon. Big dreams. No fear. I was at the wheel of life.

And I was in the driver's seat.

Act

The little soul settled at the edge of heaven. For a moment he absorbed its glow. He could rest for a while, so he directed his attention back toward his body.

"I see you're working today." God appeared and waited for today's topic.

"I'm old enough now, so I'm thinking about my purpose. I can influence my mind at times, especially when I start thinking about the future. I'm planning how to get my mind's attention."

"Yes, you are growing up. And yet through your childhood you've already been presented with great questions. Fear, loneliness, love. I've shown how you can be part of the experience of others. As a soul, able to influence your life, how will you use this experience to accomplish your purpose?"

"Exactly what I am working on. Over the next few years, I will be making decisions that set up so much of my path. What career, where to live, who to marry. If I can stay connected with my mind, I think this can be a grand adventure. There's so little time, and I need to get my own attention more often."

God chuckled, "I guess I'll save eternity for later. Would you like a little help to stir things up while you're awake?"

"What do you mean?"

"Little Soul, do you forget to ask? I don't have any great floods planned, but it's not hard to push a few choice moments into one life. What do you think? A special girl? A broken leg? A new idea? By coincidence

or accident? How would you like Me to help you on your journey?"

The little soul thought for a moment. "Every choice I make will send my path another direction. How can I be sure what to ask for? If I meet the wrong girl, go to the wrong school, pick the wrong fight, I'll end up somewhere I didn't want. I think I need some character building experiences, but I need opportunity too. Then again, I need to be awake enough to seize it and not in a love sick stupor."

God teased him a bit more, "Maybe circumstances should change. A great storm wipes out the town. Are you a hero? Are you a victim? How would you like it? Shall I send a plague? Loved ones to die? Fight the good fight to survive? Aren't there character building opportunities in tragedies? What do you think?"

"Dear God no, I won't ask for calamities that affect others. Especially not just to improve myself."

"All things affect others. A kiss can start a family, or cause a crucifixion. You are thinking a bit too hard." God paused for a moment to let the little soul think. "You may ask for anything, but what must you do to fulfill your purpose?"

"Dear God. I need to pay attention. I cannot choose every step."

"Good answer. I expect you to think and plan and work at it. Both your mind and soul need to make the effort. As your journey continues, if you pay attention, you will recognize My plans. You will find joy in your part. You will make your adventure much more interesting. Opportunities are neither as you expect or plan. Sometimes, you will embark upon things that just

don't work out. And then, things will fall in to place. Learn to pay attention. Pray, ask, and be grateful. When you see My plan, act!"

Racoon Riches

The winter months in northwest Iowa were interminable stretches of boredom. Long cold dark nights, four network TV stations, and homework. Having reached an age of sufficient independence to wander the countryside with guns in pursuit of game, we mourned the closing of hunting season. In this desperate situation, a remarkable new pastime emerged. We discovered coon hunting.

It began when Glenn returned from visiting extended family in the Ozark mountains over Christmas and came home having discovered coon hunting. The most significant item was the dog he brought home. I don't know how the dog survived the sub-freezing temperatures riding amongst the family belongings in the garden cart towed behind the family sedan. There were discrepant stories of how the dog even appeared. But the dog became the ultimate weapon in defeating deep winter boredom.

The scheme was simple. Raccoons are nocturnal scavengers. One goes out into the countryside at night, turns the dog loose, and follows the barking and baying oncc a raccoon is treed. Come up to the tree, shine a spotlight into the limbs, and shoot the raccoon. Coon hides are thickest, and therefore bring the best prices, in the dead of winter. Coon hunting was in the dark, on cold winter nights, with dogs, friends, guns, and lost in the wilderness. In the dreary dead of winter, this is perfection.

Coon hunting required crossing a lot of fences,

and you never knew whose property you might be hunting on. At midnight in February at ten degrees, we received few complaints. No one bothers looking outside if they hear a bunch of baying dogs and gunshots in the woodlot behind the barn at midnight. Anyone would conclude it was just coon hunters. Or perhaps the Sheriff had already followed tracks through dark cold fields in the early hours only to discover coon hunters. Or perhaps he didn't. We never heard a complaint over the sound of the wind, the shouts, the dogs, and the guns.

There was always an aim of conducting commerce in hides. We re-lived a piece of history, imagining ourselves to be fur trappers hauling hides to a local trader's den. There we would trade hides for local currency, drinks, and some conversation. However, coon hunting was so much fun that an evening jaunt through the countryside might include ten friends. Splitting the proceeds left little after ammunition costs.

After a long winter of coon hunts with little cash to show, but a lifetime of stories, we were driving to school one morning and saw a big old raccoon laying alongside the road.

"Oh, man! I'll bet it still has its winter hide!" We stopped and collected the precious road kill and put it in the truck. Maybe it was rigor mortis, or maybe it was frozen, but it was stiff, deformed, and broken. I suppose road kill can be like that, but the hide was all there.

At school, we opened the trunk and showed off our prize roadkill to the curious and jealous sportsmen in my class. It was a big 'ol coon splayed out filling the trunk. Arguments ensued over the quality of the hide and the price it would fetch after the evidence of tire damage was brushed and groomed away.

On the way home, we determined it would be necessary to defrost the critter before we could skin it. Racing home, we snuck the roadkill into the house, and down to the basement to thaw out. The house rule was we had to clean our kills outside. But we had never tried to skin a frozen carcass before. Overnight in the basement should solve the problem, and we planned to sneak it back outside to be skinned the next day. As luck would have it, we were up against the weekend, and mom stayed around the house. It wasn't until Monday we could sneak the coon back outside. The plan almost worked. There was a bit of a rank odor. The kind of odor you would be afraid of breathing too much of or it would burn your nostrils. The kind of odor you were afraid would never leave your clothes. The kind of odor that made you wonder why paint was still hanging on the walls. It didn't matter though, because Mom only went to the basement when her pantry thinned out.

We moved to the garage and began to peel the pelt off the carcass. Other than frequent breaks to step out for fresh air, regular progress was occurring until Mom pulled in. Somehow, she forgot to take a deep breath before getting out of the car, and made the mistake of drawing a full dose of the misty rotten-old-hide-and-gut scented air in the garage. Air thickened with putrefying elements takes some gradual getting used to, and the sudden shock to Mom's system turned her slight five-foot stature into a raging monster. Two six foot teenage boys and a raccoon were out in the chilly March afternoon.

Becoming a professional purveyor of hides presented a few problems. Our prize hide was outdoors and not allowed to enter ANY building on the property. The prize hide had to be stored away from thieves or other critters that might want to eat it! We wrapped it in kraft paper, tied it up, and hoisted it up the flag pole for the night. We were sure it was safe from bears, but not so sure about thieves. It would have to do.

Comparing notes with the other professional fur traders at school, it became clear we had missed the prime trading season. Hide prices were dropping like a rock. The best course of action would be to drop the hide in a freezer until the next winter when pelts would trade at even higher prices. The plan was better than owning stocks, or real estate which always go up, but we couldn't afford.

Mom had not recovered from odiferous shock. The proposal to use her freezer to store our precious hide right next to the fresh sirloin reignited apoplectic fits. And so, when the chips are down, call grandma. It turned out, grandma had an old freezer out on the porch for keeping the "boys'" venison. As long as the coon was in a plastic bag, no problem. The hide deposited, we could wait for prices to rise.

Later that summer, tragedy struck. Another raccoon, this time a live one, made its way into grandma's back porch and made a mess. Overlooked in the cleanup was the unplugged cord to the freezer. A hundred pounds of rotting venison buried the precious coon hide. Grandma couldn't take the smell and needed someone to take the freezer to the dump. She took a shot at cleaning it, but the fumes had overcome her.

Reviewing the tragedy with friends, my buddy Eddie said his mom would take the freezer if he cleaned it out. Deal and done, the next day began with a project at hand. Six strapping teenagers, a four-wheel-drive pickup, a two-hundred pound freezer on an elevated porch with a hundred pounds of rotting venison inside. Grandma warned us to not open the lid until we were five miles out of town. While Eddie's mom was inside that limit Grandma didn't know. Managing the freezer onto the truck had been an ordeal, but removing the porch rail put the truck bed at just the right height. Grandma needed a new screen door anyway, and a few new grooves on the already worn wooden planks added fresh character. Working one problem at a time, we had not considered delivery of the freezer. Eddie's place didn't have a raised porch. Everyone agreed removing the hundred pounds of venison would make the job easier. Everyone also agreed Eddie had volunteered to do it, so we all left, figuring, "job well done." I reminded Eddie our coon hide was sealed in a plastic bag, and still worth a lot of dough, so when he found it to please pick it out.

Eddie delivered one scoop shovel of venison from the freezer to a garbage can. He puffed, ran around the house, lay down on the grass, and breathed deep fresh breaths. After a few minutes, he took another deep breath, and ran back for another scoop-full. All afternoon, Eddie went back and forth, holding his breath, scooping rotten venison, and escaping to fresh air to recharge. It never occurred to him his mom, Lillie, may not want the freezer.

Lillie was a loud type of woman. Not gaudy load, or dressed in bright colors loud. She was ‘make a big noise’ kind of loud. She was often a champion at the county fair husband calling contest. We lived a quarter mile down the road from Eddie. When Lillie got home, she found the truck, the freezer, and two garbage cans filled with rot. There are a lot of smells included in the fresh air on an Iowa farm. But a rotting dead animal smell is not tolerated long. “EDDIE!!! EDDIE get this pile of crap out of here RIGHT NOW.” Poor Eddie was wheezing on the grass in the back yard and lacked the strength to roll over. Lillie came running around the house holding her nose, tripped over Eddie, and let out a scream heard in our living room over the theme song for Bonanza.

We stepped outside and took a look. “Want to go over?”

“Not really. I can kind of smell it from here.”

“Yeah, nothing much we could do anyway. Just hose it all down I suppose, and heck, they can do that.”

“Do you think he found the coonskin?”

“That’s right, we could go help, I suppose.”

“Naw, Bonanza’s starting”

That afternoon, Eddie closed the lid, never to be opened again. The garbage cans were carried to a ditch where he dumped them and ran. The truck went to the dump, and the freezer pushed off. Coonskin riches slipped through our fingers.

Monte Carlo

Car companies work hard to come up with distinctive names for their models. Evocative images of unique lifestyles that are glamorous, mysterious, exciting, or downright better than anybody else are produced from just the right name.

Mitch, my best friend, in high school drove into the yard one day with a Monteee Caarloooo! And just the way he said it, Steve and I knew he was already a better person.

The Monteee Caarloooo, never shortened to "Monte", or any sort of nickname, became the preferred vehicle for group events for the next few years. While the Monteee Caarloooo was sophisticated, and glamorous, we chose it to be our ride for the once in a lifetime camping trip to Grey Cliff, Montana.

Our combined ages would not make a post office retirement and we had much to learn on our cross-country adventure. Did you know cars will in fact go as fast as the speedometer needle goes? Night time driving, windows down, going ninety miles-per-hour will make you deaf for a while. There are no gas stations open after two a.m. Dawn on the badlands is like a moon landing. A Harley can still go faster than a Monteee Caarloooo, but the driver can't last as long. They will sell dirty books to teenagers in Rapid City but not beer. After the first thousand antelopes, you go back to sleeping. If you drive long enough and fast enough, you can put a fresh oil change through your car in about three stops for gas.

Grey Cliff, Montana is a gas station, post office, and general store. It's one building. With the urban sprawl coming off the ranch, it may have grown by now, but at the time it was not hard getting across town. The ranch was part of a two-farm partnership that Mitch's family was half of. The Montana ranch dropped calves and pastured them. At some point, they were sent to Iowa to be marbled up and moved to market. Mitch had never been to the ranch but gained permission for us to camp there. The ranch encompassed ten square miles bordered on the south by the Yellowstone river. Lying perhaps fifty miles east of its namesake park, the river birthed from the freshest water this side of heaven.

The Monteee Caarloooo followed a pair of bare ruts around the edge of the property to the shoreline. We pitched tents, built a fire, and listened to wolves howl at the moon. Maybe they were coyotes, but the deep lonely sounds creasing the clear mountain air could be understood in ways no Iowa coyote ever inspired.

After a fine night's rest on pine cones and tree roots, and considering the previous day's journey of a thousand miles, it was decided a swim in the Yellowstone was in order. We had to be mountain men, so in we went buck naked. While we lost feeling in our submerged parts the instant they touched water, our minds kept receiving signals of great distress to the body. That fresh pure water had been snow thirty minutes prior to cascading down the mountain and cooling the shores of our campsite. The downward slope of the river would have made for a toboggan run.

But with a river in the way, we had to stand in the raging current that was driving ice crystals through our skin. We debated if we stood in the Yellowstone river and drank a warm beer if it would freeze as it reached our bellies. While they won't sell beer to minors in Rapid City, somewhere on the overnight trip beer had appeared in the trunk of the Monteee Caarloooo! We settled for putting a few six packs on a fish stringer in the river, figuring they'd be ready in a minute or two.

We emerged, clean from the knees down and ready for more adventure. It turned out, the ranch had a canoe. We approached uncle Bane at the ranch to see if we could borrow the canoe. "What, oh that thing? Sure, it washed up here one day. Some fool tried to ride that river I suppose. Nothin' but rapids for fifty miles in either direction. Some idiot thought he could ride a canoe in it. Is your mother happy you're gone? I know your dad won't care. Go ahead, I couldn't stop you, anyway. You might want to have a few beers before you go. Relaxes you some and improves your nerves." Uncle Bane seemed to understand young men our age, even if he had never married or had kids. I guess some folks are natural parents.

We found the canoe in a quiet backwater behind a fallen cottonwood. This was a blessing as it would allow us to get in the canoe before reaching escape velocity in the current. Mitch suggested this would be an ideal spot for our morning bath in the river. Without the torrential current we might get deeper, and maybe even get clean. We would have to get clean before getting back into his Monteee Caarloooo.

Riding a canoe on the Yellowstone just means

hanging on for as long as you can until the rocks above and below the water line scrape your knuckles or bang your head enough to make you let go. 100% of the trip was underwater. Steve and I emerged on the wrong side of the river. We looked across to the other shore in astonishment. Mitch had the canoe on the other shore. It was just luck that the rope on the canoe had strangled his left arm above the elbow and dragged him like an anchor down river before catching an overhanging tree branch and snagging the whole assemblage. Mitch would always get lucky that way.

Steve and I had to cross the thirty-foot-wide torrent. We agreed it was better hanging your head out the window of the Monteee Carloooo at high speed than dipping it in the river because your brain doesn't freeze so bad.

The next year Mitch moved and got a real job in another town, "up north". He was part of local law enforcement and the two hundred citizens of Lost Prairie would be safer with Mitch and his sidearm. Mitch worked the night shift as the local sheriff couldn't work all twenty-four hours a day. This worked great, because Mitch could go fishing and hunt pheasants all day, and sleep in his squad car all night. Steve and I made our way up north to spend a weekend and enjoy some fishing.

Saturday afternoon on the lake Mitch sheepishly announced we would have to pull out early because he had a friend getting married and he was the best man. Having almost caught our limit, we decided we were OK with a wedding as long as there was food afterward. Arriving a little early we slipped our "good" T-shirts on and sauntered in to find out what Mitch's duties would be for the afternoon. That's when we met Eric, the groom.

Eric was descended from the Vikings, the Minnesota ones and the real ones. Give him a skull cap, and a bearskin and he would have been right at home in the stadium or the fifteenth century, either way. Standing about six feet six, he wore a grin as wide as Mitch's head. "I see you brought the ushers," he said, looking at Steve and me. "I was supposed to get ushers, and I forgot. Linda would kick my ass if I forgot ushers. Don't worry about the clothes, she'll just be glad to see ushers."

Gee, what could we say? "Hello Eric, nice to meet you. Will that be bride's side or groom's side?" The crowd was manageable. Eric had forgotten to tell his family he was getting married. He was sure he would let them know about becoming grandparents sometime shortly after the wedding. The crowd amounted to the bride's mother and sister and six friends. Steve and I each had to decide between sitting with six young females or the groom's side. I'm not sure if Steve or I had the better view. I suppose it depended on what you were looking at. Afterward we all went down to a supper club with a wooden ceiling and lots of mounted deer heads. Mitch let Eric and Linda borrow the Monteee Caarloooo and we walked home.

A couple months later it was duck season and Eric had his priorities straightened out again. He and Mitch rode down in the Monteee Caarloooo to our place. We ventured into the great Missouri river floodplain to hunt ducks. Hunting ducks was new to Mitch, Steve, and I, but Eric was an enthusiast. He had an uncle with a duck blind next to a flooded ditch along a field. It was the perfect place, and the perfect day.

Still young and learning, there is much to know about duck hunting. A perfect day consists of freezing rain mixed with snow from low clouds because the ducks will be flying within range. You get to your duck blind well before daylight while the ducks are on the ground and won't take off. Then you crawl into a wet muddy hole, half full of water, and start quacking like a duck when the sun doesn't come up. You face the wind, which means in western Iowa you will let the wind blow the ducks off the field and into your line of fire. Some folks believe ice fishing is insanity. Chopping holes, sitting on ice, believing frozen fish will wake up and bite a hook baited with wax worms. It seems quite sane after duck hunting.

With a grey sensation that sunrise had occurred, the ducks got up and started flying south as fast as they could. Warm sand and margaritas in Mexico, the ducks had more brains than we did. I think I saw ducks wearing sunglasses. They would just stretch out their wings and the wind would blow them to Mexico. There were a few lazy sorts showing off by flying on their backs with their legs crossed. They corrected our duck calls while whizzing by. We shot behind ducks all morning. I know we saw some smiling and flipping us their middle feather on the way by. As our muddy hole began to freeze over we crawled out and decided it had been a good day because we saw lots of ducks. We reached the Monteee Caarloooo, removed our coveralls and boots and put them in plastic bags before settling in to our sophisticated ride back home. We felt like better people, just saying the name. Monteee Caarloooo!

It's Complicated

The little soul went looking for company, "Hello Mom. How's the edge of heaven today?"

"It's fine. I enjoy it here."

"How is it going down there?"

"I'm forgetting things. I don't remember your father all the time, and it hurts him. We are getting old, you know."

"Why don't you ask God to change this."

"Oh, we talk often. I spend a lot of time here now because I sleep quite a lot. Your dad worries so about things. You see, he's afraid right now. He's never been alone. He's getting angry and confused and doesn't know what to do."

"You mean your condition is part of dad's journey? Why would you do this?"

"I can assure you it's not my idea. But I am at peace with this, and your father's soul is as well."

"Why must it be like this? A beautiful life together, torn by disease. The family confused and uncertain. What good comes from this?"

"I have asked these questions, too. I have also visited with many souls here at the edge, concerned with their lives, their purpose. Some worry if they have lived up to God's plans. We cannot fail in completing God's purpose. We can only fail in seeing how we are part of His plan. We are given chances to do more or less.

"I am almost ready to come home now for good. Your father won't be far behind me. This end of my journey has much more to do with others than myself. I

linger in order for God to offer others an occasion to experience another element in His plan."

"Am I to take every chance God gives me?"

"Oh dear, no. God is far too creative for us to keep up. Make your choices, make good ones, and make the most of them. You will prepare a fine gift for God. You already have, I can tell."

"Mom," they looked below, "why does God's plan make dad upset? "

"It is His will somehow. I expect your father still needed to learn something about faith. I know he knows love. It's hard to watch from here."

The little soul drifted along the edge to be alone, but God was with him. "As I grow up, it gets harder, doesn't it?"

"More complicated, perhaps. The challenges will increase for you. As will My blessings. I expect the most of you as your skills develop. You will bring a great gift to heaven."

"Dear God, can you help me understand while I am awake. I am sure I can do better, but I just can't think clearly."

"Why is that?"

"The family is changing, growing up, leaving, dying. There are new people I meet that I don't understand. There are pressures for living. The distractions are everywhere."

"Little Soul, I hear your prayer. I will give you a nudge soon. A moment to awaken your thoughts. It will be just enough for you to move along your path."

Good Luck

A warm summer morning. Dad had gone to work early running a load of cattle for someone. There were always trucking jobs filling the small gaps between farm work. Chores were done and a morning shower reminded my stomach breakfast was overdue. Bacon and French toast with real maple syrup. Well past sunup, the birds had calmed down. Livestock was murmuring on full bellies. A grassy breeze beneath high clouds betrayed the coming heat of the afternoon.

An altogether normal day. Yet a day that marked a change. I was leaving for college that morning. I knew once I left home, I would never come back. Others had told me as much. Visiting home was never the same.

Mom clucked over a pie crust she had to flip. Big sis was already off to her college. Steve was at preseason football practice for high school. A perfect normal day added to my melancholy. Anxiety nibbled at my soul.

My path had been determined by others. One fine autumn day a year before, principal Burns called me to his office. I was sitting in chemistry class when Mr. Burns' voice crackled over the intercom summoning my name. Enduring a gauntlet of looks, I made my way out the door and down the hall. Arriving, Mr. Burns and Mr. Galloway, the guidance counselor, were sharing a smile over something one had remarked.

"There you are, come on in here," Mr. Burns was in an odd mood. I felt like the pig right before the roast. "We've got an opportunity for you. You are one lucky young man! Are you familiar with the Ag-may fertilizer company? They're over by the river terminal. They've offered one engineering scholarship for a senior this year. Mr. Galloway has elected you as the most likely to complete an engineering degree in your class, so you will receive this award this year. You'll get to attend Iowa State University next fall and Ag-may will cover your tuition. You must come up with room and board, but hey son, your folks feed you every night anyway, don't they?"

"Yeah, sure." I had been thinking about working as a carpenter for a contractor for a few years, and then maybe setting off on my own.

"That's great son. Go home and let your folks know. They'll be proud of you when we announce your scholarship at the spring arts and awards night. Everyone will know before then, but this will be special. We've never had someone get an industrial sponsored scholarship. Yes, you are one lucky fellow!"

And so, I went home and told the folks. "I'm not sure." I told them. "I was thinking about being a carpenter."

"That's just fine." Mom replied. "You can be a carpenter right after you finish college. This is exciting for you. You are one lucky young man!"

It was settled. I didn't visit the college, or sit in on a class. No weekend stay to see if I liked it. Paperwork was filled out by the guidance counselor. A letter arrived in the mail with a day to report, a parking lot to use, and a building to show up at. A great shadowy unknown hung around with me all year. I had papers. My path settled. I wondered what engineers did. I was going to be one.

A ghostly monkey rode my back through senior year. Its haunting coolness wormed its way into early morning moments, dull afternoons on the tractor, and mundane minutes during study hall. When summer came, the grim reality of a sharp unknown developed continuous unease. Life came marching at me. One lucky fellow.

With the car loaded, I gave mom a hug and said goodbye. Goodbye to mom. Goodbye to childhood. Goodbye to home. And off I went.

The towers were spotted at a distance as I approached the edge of town. Monolithic residence halls grouped to dominate the horizon. Home was never so far away. I followed the instructions. I parked. I showed up, signed up, and unpacked to an 8x12 room with built in furniture. Life had changed. Off to class.

The instructors in college are a bit more profound in their own narrow specialties. Most of my professors were passionate and fun and completely nuts. Every course was taught with vigor. Five courses at a time, I was in deep. I began to figure out the actual purpose of college. In preparation for adulthood, every bit of childhood joy and freedom was to be squashed until forgotten.

Life was relearned as a serious venture. Introduced to pressure, deadlines, and stress, failure was not an option. Yet our professors routinely informed us that two out of three would never become engineers. I had never considered a "plan B." In fact, I had never considered "plan A." As the only option underway, it remained the only option. Study, get serious, and learn math like Newton, Gauss, and Pascal.

After getting accustomed to the routine, it occurred to me that not all the students were handling things well. Instant reversions to childhood occurred. Denial of reality was common. Denial of homework was effective for a semester, two at most. Declarations of freedom followed by breaking the law and a night without freedom was routine. Drinking one's stress away was a communal lesson shared amongst students. Stress therapy began on Friday afternoon and ended in missing church Sunday morning.

There were other students content at a desk in the basement of a building under dim lights in front of green screens. These would become "techie" people or researchers someday. While captive on campus, they were avoiding the rambunctious happenings occurring in the dorms.

But a few normal people kept showing up in class during the week. The cauldron in which childhood dreams were distilled to the thin gruel of careers could not ruin a tenacious few. One of these was George. George was invariable about his daily demeanor. Homework was done. Lunch was that on the menu without complaint. Bedtime was before midnight, and classes started at eight. George was the first thing that resembled family since leaving home.

After a month of adjusting to college, George and I had become good friends. We went to class, we studied, we ate, we studied. One day, George had an idea, "Hey, we should do something."

"What?"

"I don't know. Just something."

"Do we have time? I've got physics problems to figure out before Monday."

"Let's get up Saturday morning when everyone else is sleeping and drive somewhere." And we did. We found the country, now burnt with the crisp frosts of fall. A river with stones to throw. A small town with a quiet hardware store, a busy café, and a smelly gas station. We stopped at a used car dealer and admired how well the discarded had been cleaned up.

I went to church the next morning and sat in a pew. A familiar song, a sermon, contented families. Bittersweet familiar moments. An enduring substitute for home. All grown up. One lucky fellow.

Seneca, a Roman Philosopher, is credited with coining the phrase, "Luck is when preparation meets with opportunity." It's a fancy way of saying, "Work your butt off, and maybe something will come along." But I met luck once, and his name was Merlin. And while Merlin prepared no more than anyone else, his luck served up opportunity in rare portions.

George and I were off on a Saturday morning excursion and had stopped for a late breakfast. While our classmates slept in, we had discovered the world was wide open to us. Our ventures that morning had turned up a series of rough draws and creeks bordered by cornfields. We were thinking about the upcoming pheasant season and were lamenting our lack of practice. Engineering school was sapping our talent for shooting straight. Accustomed to stepping from the back door at home past the windbreak of maples, pines, and spruces, we had our own wide open range. Shooting through a dozen boxes of shells before opening day, we looked forward to limits of roast pheasants. But here we were, six weeks into engineering school, and no place to shoot.

Our lamentations reached above the sound of pouring coffee and frying bacon. The only other patron in the café at that hour spun off his stool at the counter and pulled up a chair at our table. "How would you like some shooting practice?" Merlin had the mature confidence of forty yet sported the beard of a sixteen-year-old refusing to shave his first sprouts. "My dad has a cattle farm just down the road here. We've got a terrible pigeon problem, and we'd like them thinned out a bit. Are you boys any good with a shotgun or do you just talk about it?" The university didn't like us keeping guns in the dorms, so they were convenient and ready in the trunk of the car. He bought our breakfast, and we followed him home.

Merlin's dad raised cattle like God used to raise buffalo on the plains. You could have walked on their backs for a quarter mile at a time. Great herds of black Angus. Market ready stocky beasts built like rail cars on legs. Hungry new calves no bigger than sled strapped Huskies. Hundreds of cattle in all sizes, black as midnight with an occasional white splotch peeking from a few faces. Merlin pointed to another impressive collection. "Out there on the hill, we just moved a bunch in from there. See the pigeons?" The hillside moved, and bits of it fluttered. "Pigeons. They just sit around and wait. When we move the grain trucks down to fill the chutes that flock will land in the corn and help themselves. They bother the cattle and steal our grain. My guess is there's a thousand or so. Hope you brought enough shells."

The shooting was spectacular. Once startled, the flock circled and buzzed the farm, determined to never leave the good charity and sustenance of the cattle farm. Two hours of continuous pigeon shooting had sharpened our eyes, quickened our reflexes, and bruised our shooting shoulders. Exhausted of ammunition, we cased our guns and went to thank Merlin. A busy worker pointed us toward a likely barn and we entered to find a remodeled set of offices. The décor included polished wood, stainless steel benches, and office chairs designed for the cockpit of a fighter jet. Merlin was working at a bench with snarls of wires, tools, and electronic bits.

"Thanks for the chance to shoot pigeons Merlin. If it's OK, we'll come back again."

"Any time."

"What'cha working on?"

"Oh this? We're building subassemblies for computers. I got mad at the computer store a couple months ago because we went through three machines that failed. The sales guy told me they all had the same problem, but they were coming from overseas by the boat load. There was no chance to fix the problem at the factory before thousands of units shipped. He wasn't even sure the factory knew of the problem. But he knew precisely what it was. I offered to fix his units, and he opened his dock to a hundred and fifty returned units.

"I fixed those, then he sent me some more. I volunteered to fix his new ones before he sold them and he sent me two hundred more. Now they're shipping them in from all over the country. Takes about ten minutes apiece. We unbox them, clip this item out, and solder this little piece in there. I'm getting fifty bucks apiece. Truck comes every day. I've got three guys helping, too."

Engineering students are good at math. Money is simple math. "Wow, that's real money."

"Yeah, but they're happy because we're saving their butts. Almost everything we work on right now is brand new. Someday they'll figure it out. For now, we're riding the PC revolution."

It seemed Merlin had stumbled into a bit of good luck. It's good to hang around with lucky people. We met him for breakfast the next week.

"Hey, you guys are a couple engineers. What do you think about this? There's this new product called oriented strand board. It's supposed to replace plywood, but it's basically crap." We were familiar with it and agreed. "When I flunked out of chemical engineering, we were studying surface tension. You know how this wood is made from pieces of chopped fibers of all sizes. Each size piece causes the surface tension to vary so the glue strength varies too much. Look at this piece I made here." Knowing he was eating breakfast with engineers, he correctly assumed we loved to talk shop.

"That's a much better piece. You can tell right off. What'd you do?"

"Oh, I just sprayed the glue in using six variations on the glue. I mix them so they stay separated like oil and water, and I get more variation in droplet size which affects surface tension. This way, each bit of wood fiber gets some glue that sticks to it well. When you compress it, problem solved!" Merlin had few limits for problems he enjoyed tackling. We made regular treks to his farm as time allowed.

After four tough years of courses, final exams, and senior projects, George and I received diplomas. Merlin came to graduation to shake our hands. "Merlin! Glad you could make it! Haven't seen you in months. How's it going?"

"Oh, I've been busy with the glue project. We set some mixing tanks up out at the farm. You know a truck load of this, a few buckets of that. Not much to it. But we gotta keep it flowing. We're doing two million a month now."

"Two million what? Gallons?"

"No, dollars. Heck there's no way we could do two million gallons. I'd need a new barn! So anyway, you guys got degrees, congratulations. Got jobs yet?"

George and I found jobs just far enough apart that we could visit each other and Merlin every few months. We remained friends, and Merlin remained lucky. Having discovered overtime, report writing, and the glamor of business travel, I yearned for visits to Merlin's farm. Still protected by surrounding herds of cattle, novel secrets and experiments percolated in the lab.

"I like the new concrete drive. Quite a spread out here."

"Oh, had to. The glue trucks would get stuck."

"What'cha working on?"

"Hey, you know that surface tension problem? Well I was thinking. And you know, I can vary the thickness of glue on stuff. So, I borrowed some fertilizer from dad and started playing around. You know, with a water-soluble coating I can make time released fertilizer. That's what the new barn across the drive is going up for. Need to make ten thousand before the end of the year."

"Dollars?"

"No, bags. That's about six million dollars. How are you doin?"

"Hey, I got a four percent raise already. I get to fly to places like Cleveland on business."

Merlin continued through random projects in every corner. "See this? I found out you can weld engineered fabric materials. This will make perfect sterile metering tubes. And it's cheap. Use it and throw it.

"And then it turns out certain bacteria will eat oil. This is my oil remediation kit. I have a guy in Europe who's launching sales over there. You know how to make hot water for northern greenhouses with no energy? I have a fish tank over here. I can raise a four-pound bass in six weeks. Cat food companies are looking at it. Ever notice how sand sticks to everything?"

Merlin had the knack to see a simple problem, find a solution, and turn it into a business. He lived in engineering heaven. "How's George doing?"

"Oh, George is getting married." Merlin's face fell. His body slumped, the energy from moments before spent. With a breath, he mustered a response, "That's cool. Hey, you got a girl too. You are the luckiest guys on the planet. How are you and your girl?"

It was my turn to go speechless. I assembled my own underwhelming response between confused brain cells, "Ah, OK. I took her out to a hockey game last week and bought her a Snickers bar."

"See what I mean? You are one lucky fella. I wish I had a girl," and Merlin fell into an uncharacteristic mope. My lucky friend thought I was the lucky one. "Hey, do you think you could help find me a date?" Merlin began to see his problem and was processing solutions.

"I'm not so sure."

"How about the university? You must know tons of girls over there."

"Well Merlin, it *is* Iowa State. The first ten thousand students are engineers. The next ten thousand are studying agriculture. If you can't do those, you go over to the business school. Get the picture? I mean, about eight guys for every girl over there."

"OK, where do single girls hang out so I can find one?" I promised to ask around.

George's fiancé seemed a logical source. She was a woman, so she should know where they hung out. Churches, rummage sales, and baby showers didn't offer much hope for Merlin. "Why don't you guys just take a couple girls to the movies?" The only actionable option, we went to the movies. We forgot to ask girls ahead of time, so we bought our tickets, and hung out by the door waiting for some before the feature started.

"Are you girls taken?" Merlin went for the direct inquiry as three young ladies slipped by with horrified looks.

"Merlin, maybe try a nice greeting first."

"OK." Another approached, "You're a fine-looking gal. Want to see a movie?"

"Gee since I bought a ticket, maybe I will." A confident one breezed by.

"No luck yet, I guess. Let's just go in."

Two women of sufficient age to claim experience at killing a few husbands came smiling up to us. "You boys looking for dates?" Veterans of the dating scene, they didn't waste time. They had mastered the art of make-up to keep us guessing if there were scars anywhere. Yet their attire left little guess work for their basic structural features.

Unexpected, unprepared, and polite enough to respect our elders, Merlin slipped up and said, "Yeah, well yes, but...."

"Oh, good. Come sit with us! This is so exciting. We were kind of hoping to find some nice young college boys tonight." Aghast at our luck, but unable to withdraw, they each took an arm, and lead us in to the theater. Merlin and I sat together, with our cultured escorts on each side blocking the exits.

I leaned over and whispered to Merlin, "Hey, what's the movie?" Merlin had purchased tickets, and I hadn't seen what was showing.

"Something about a soldier coming home from the war and finding out his sweetheart thought he was dead. Sounded like a good war movie."

"Oh crap. This is a tear jerking melodramatic sappy three-way love story. What are we going to do?"

"Well, first get your hand off my leg."

"Merlin, other side. That's not my hand. Your date is migrating into your seat. Beat her back, the movie is just starting." We endured the chick flick, but our companions had become attached to us. With fingernails embedded through my sleeves I was sure the nail polish was printing a tattoo.

"How would you gals like to go out to my place? It's only a mile down the road." I thought Merlin had lost touch with reality.

"Ah, Merlin, come again? I mean these fine ladies need to be going home."

"Oh, we'd love to. We've got nowhere we need to be tonight, or even tomorrow morning." I detected a wink from the eyelash brushing my cheek. I had been looking for an escape route, but Merlin had wrapped the chain and snapped the lock. We were caught.

As Merlin's date accompanied him under the steering wheel, I decided I would have to share a seatbelt with my date in the back seat. I knew I could run a mile in the dark, but remained concerned about leaving Merlin. A moment of optimism occurred as we pulled in. "What's that smell?"

"Oh, we've got about four hundred head of cattle right now. Just moved a hundred off the orchard side of the house. It's not bad most of the time, but the wind is out of the east and we haven't cleaned up that yard." Our dates sat up, but didn't let go. We stepped from the car into the moist aromatic summer evening. The black herd shifted in the dark night. The quiet murmur of cattle framed an expulsive snort next to us. A shriek began in my right ear and came out my left. My date was startled by the snorting black monster in the night. My temporary deafness prevented me from noticing.

"What's the matter?" Merlin was genuine. There was nothing to notice, other than a scream in the night.

"What is that? What's that beast out there?"

"Oh, that's just cattle. They're fine. But we shouldn't spook them. They might stampede. They won't see fences in the dark, and then we'll be all over the county collecting cattle." We moved to Merlin's workshop. "Hey, I was thinking while we were in the movie about something I'm working on you gals might like." The shop had its normal collection of projects coloring the air with smells of burnt dust, ozone, and solvents. A heady mix to get the mind buzzing. "It occurred to me while that poor guy in the movie had part of a leg shot off, remember?" The ladies had blank expressions. "So, here's a mechanism I'm working on for a self-leveling chair. I'll bet one of these could work for a guy's leg. Kind of self-leveling mechanism so the guy wouldn't fall over. What do you think?" Merlin had killed the movie romance, reducing a tragic storyline to a problem solved. I began to think he was on to something.

"Then, remember how his buddies were all messed up from mustard gas in the war? I've got this bag balm you rub on cow udders. This is great stuff. With a little colorant, I'll bet this would clear up those guys' complexion." Merlin kept going. His date had detached. The red claw marks were still visible on George's neck, but he no longer seemed to notice. "Now you know how they ran out of gasoline that one night? I'll never run out of gas. See this bulb? It's filled with a special fluid that illuminates when the vapor pressure in the gas tank changes." The girls had vanished. Merlin stopped.

"What was that all about?" I was perplexed at the turn of events.

"I had to test a theory of mine. Every time I bring

a girl home she runs off. I'm not sure what it is about this place, but someday I'll have to move away if I ever want to get a girl."

"You never know Merlin," I said. "Some-day you might get lucky."

The Last Year

There was a day I realized I left the home had grown up in. It was years after I packed up and moved out on my own. Home changed from the place I lived, to that place I went back to for holidays, vacations, and family gatherings.

One morning I awoke in my childhood bed resting in that space between dreaming and awareness. There was a baby and a toddler crawling on me and a woman lying there next to me telling me it was 'my turn' because she wanted some sleep. It's a strange way to wake up. I wandered downstairs, and there was mom making eggs for breakfast. That may seem normal to most, but in my house mom didn't make eggs, dad did. She was a great cook, an expert at deserts. She might make breakfast food for dinner, something like French toast and scrambled eggs served for supper. But mom never made eggs for breakfast. It was an odd sort of day. Something was different about being home.

I stepped outside to the deck and felt for something familiar. My soul seemed unsettled.

At the end of countless days, we sat on the deck at the back of the house. Mom and dad lived on a hill in Iowa that overlooked the Missouri river floodplain and deep into Nebraska. For many long summer evenings, we lingered there as thunderstorms rolled up and over us, followed by rainbows and sunshine. The wind always blew.

I went back inside and Stevie had shown up

with a woman and a bunch of kids. A feeling persisted, something was different about being home. Stevie and I poked around in the barn. The cows and chickens were long gone. The hay was no longer fresh. The smells no longer grabbed us. Did I hear something? Were those soft sounds of contented livestock or timeless echoes? Off the edge of the barn we surveyed the crumbling remains of an old treehouse and dared each other to make the climb. Stumps stood in the orchard between a few shaggy unpruned apple trees.

Things had changed. The deck was still a favorite gathering spot and dad had learned how to grill. The jump from frying eggs to grilling steaks was not that hard. Grilling came with a view and maybe a beer or two. Mom had given up the baking of massive roasts, stuffing birds, and frying wild game. She remained an excellent dessert chef, pleasing the throng of grandchildren with home-made sweets the adults would have preferred to avoid but devoured with delight.

Dad, having been in the army, would pull out the “field glasses” that most folks called binoculars. On evenings, we would peer at towns and grain elevators stretching forty or fifty miles into Nebraska. At the edge of the deck the acreage dropped off down a hillside. In the valley and across the pond another steep hillside rose but not high enough to block the view of the long horizon. We watched wildlife and livestock and the occasional wayward neighbor kid crossing the far hillside. This late afternoon we sat on the deck and the countryside was serving up the normal dose of pastoral Americana entertainment. That was until the coyote appeared!

When a coyote appears, you must stop everything and shoot at it. It's a rule somewhere. If you are pushing the limits of your pickup down a gravel road late for a high school football game, and a coyote runs across your path, you stop, grab the guns, and shoot at it! It's a rule! If you are picking corn and you see a coyote running along the ridge, you stop, pull the gun out from behind the seat and shoot at it. It's a rule! So, there we were watching the evening unwind and a coyote trots out along the hillside across the pond. Dad said in a voice that couldn't be heard, "Careful now, let's sneak inside and I'll get my 7mm."

The "7mm" was dad's "French army rifle". When dad was eighteen, he and a million other guys got to take the great walking tour of Europe in 1944. He never talked about it. They walked across France and half of Germany, and somewhere in a ditch in Europe dad found an old French army rifle. There were no markings of manufacture or type. The barrel and action had a patina of rubbed rust. The stock was cracked but the cracked parts were so old it looked like it was made that way. Somehow dad got it home, but he had never shot it. Now, we had a coyote across the valley, and the only gun in the house that could shoot that far (maybe) was the "7mm"!

We didn't want to scare the coyote off, so dad set up to shoot from inside the house, out the sliding patio doors, with a clear view across the valley. He improvised a gun rest from an old Coleman cooler. A member of the furniture family we grew up on, it had a steel shell, rusty scratches, and bumper stickers pasted to it from Mount Rushmore. He laid down on the dining room floor, dropped the old 7mm across the cooler, and flipped up the rear sight. “What do you think boys, about four-hundred yards?” We agreed that seemed right, and he lined up for the shot.

I took a moment, as dad sighted in, to consider. Here was the main genetic link to my intelligence, laying on the dining room floor, ready to shoot a fifty-year-old gun, plucked out of a ditch, never been fired, with questionable manufacture, and using even more questionable ammunition. But, it’s a coyote and, it’s A RULE. I took a step back, and pressed the field glasses up to my eyes. I figured I would get a good view of the action, and they might protect my eyes from the probable shrapnel that would come my way.

Ka…wooooouuumppphhffft!!!!! Holy expletive! The shock wave from the gun blast penetrated right through us and reverberated back as it bounced off the walls. Our ears rung, our eyes cried, our knees went weak. Now and then, you learn something from experience, and I am happy to share this one with you. “DON’T FIRE LARGE CALIBER HIGH-POWERED RIFLES IN THE HOUSE.” That’s a freebie so you need not learn it the hard way.

Dad was lying on the floor, one big smile with his glasses laying somewhere else, “Did I get him?” It was a great shot. A plume of dust puffed up on the hillside immediately above the coyote. Somehow, the proximity of a supersonic projectile changes the local laws of physics. The coyote levitated straight into the air, hung suspended for a full second, and then returned to earth. His legs were running before he hit the dirt and he went from zero to sixty in half a second.

I learned another thing. There is a medical

condition that results from having a gun blast in the dining room traverse your body a few times. You end up rolling on the floor in fits of uncontrollable laughter, with relapses every few minutes for the rest of the evening. I know it's a legitimate medical condition, because even mom laughed. Sometimes, thirty years later, we still laugh. It's a hard condition to shake.

Later that night, we sat down on the deck again, hoping for coyotes, and settling for strange shadows dropping off distant grain elevators. In a normal conversation when dad mentioned mom he would start with, "Your mother said...." So, a comment might be, "Your mother saw a wild turkey right down that draw over there last week." But that night he was talking to me and said, "Well Darlene was telling me..."

He used my mom's name, like he was talking to a neighbor, or friend, or relative. I was dumbstruck. I didn't know what to think. It was at that moment I realized, I was a guest in my childhood home. I had finally left home.

Perhaps thirty years have passed since that day. I left home that day and began the "last year". Growing up, I saw my dad every day of every year. Three hundred sixty-five days, all twelve months of every year. But I had gone away for college and taken a job four hundred miles distant. We used to joke, "yup we both live just a mile off US highway 20, just four hundred miles down the street."

After moving and settling into a job with a new family, pilgrimages home occurred with regularity around Thanksgiving, Christmas, Easter, summer vacation, and weddings. With more babies, a new job for the new mom, and kids developing school schedules, the trips spread out. For the next ten years, I saw my dad about fifteen days a year, one hundred fifty days, or a total of five months. I saw my dad for five months of the "last year".

More kids, and music and scouts and sports and a developing career. For the subsequent decade, we still made the effort. I saw my dad for another one hundred twenty days, or about four more months of "the last year."

My dad was blessed with a long retirement. And for another ten years we still went back and forth. But Christmas and Easter were at my house now. Our own kids came home for holidays. I saw my dad for another sixty days, or perhaps two more months of the last year. Eleven months in thirty years.

Dad is now over ninety years old. He takes care of my mom as she shrinks with age. We are approaching the end of the last year. It was a long year, a good year, but it went all too fast.

A Moment

"Hello God."

"Taking a nap, I see. Contemplative little soul today?"

"Yes, I gave myself a moment today."

"Hmmm, it was time I suppose. A little early for insights, but you have lots coming up. How did it go?"

"My mind knows I'm here now."

"Yes, it's time for bigger things."

———— — ————

"Hey Steve, thought I'd give you a call. How's the kids? Is work going OK? Remember when I used to have dreams as a kid and tell you about them? Well, I had something like that yesterday, except I was wide awake. I can't get it off my mind.

"Nothing special, just in the truck sitting at a stop light. For about one full second I had a memory. Ever done that? A bit of a flashback? But it was more than a memory. It was better, even sharper than the first time.

"I remembered just a moment from when we were kids out camping. I was standing at the lake with my fishing pole. It was a Saturday morning. There was mist over the water, but the sun was warm on my chest and I could feel it! Bacon frying somewhere in camp. I could smell the earth, the camp fires, the cool humid air with corn pollen. I heard claws on bark as two squirrels chased each other up a tree trunk. And get this, I remembered looking over the water, but I also

remembered seeing the squirrels behind me like I was looking right at them. I saw the gentle lapping of waves on the shoreline and felt the mud between my toes. There was a little green frog in the water with just his nose up. I saw the park behind me, I knew where the camper was. This is the weird part, for just that moment, I could remember everything about that day.

"I even had my memories. What was going on that weekend, what you and my friends looked like, what mom and dad looked like. I knew conversations from that day, and what I was thinking about right then. I think I visited myself for a full second from when I was twelve. The thing is, the moment was so complete. I've never noticed everything going on around me in such detail. Even now I can't remember sounds and smells and memories for any given moment. How can I remember one complete second like that? And nothing special happened, so why would I remember it at all?

"Kind of like my dreams as a kid, right? But I know this was an actual memory. Do you think we remember everything in detail like this? Gosh, this was just one second. Do you think we can remember things we don't even notice at the time? Man, I could feel the whole scene.

"And then it was over, the light was still red, the radio on the same advertisement. But I can still remember all of it now. Ha! I think I've spent a couple hours thinking about that one second from years ago!

"Well, all I can say is watch every moment! Maybe next time you're in town we'll talk more."

Dad Goes Home

Steve and I were sitting on the deck. "It was a good funeral as they go. A lot of people showed up," Steve reflected on the day's events. "Yeah, I figured Dad outlived everyone he ever knew. But a lot of folks showed up. Sheriff Jim was there. I saw old Marty the well guy. He's as old as dad. Kind of odd though, sitting on the deck without dad."

"I remember dad and grandpa sitting right here on the old cistern, just like this, talking about stuff."

"Close. I think the beer is better these days." And I had to agree. The evening was still and warm and heavy. Locusts began their familiar late summer buzz. Crickets chirped from the shade underfoot. A pheasant called from the pasture. The neighbor's sheep could be heard milling about. After a time, the quiet symphony needed interruption. "I guess Dad's in a pretty good spot in heaven."

"Think so?" asked Steve, "why do people think heaven's so great?" Steve was always good at asking questions, and I suppose an answer was required.

I ruminated out loud, "Well Steve, we've both studied science and engineering now. We are familiar with the physical world. Did you ever think about this? Everything consists of molecules. The molecules are made of atoms, made of protons, neutrons, and electrons. Modern physics says the subatomic particles are common bits of energy blinking in and out of existence. The entire physical universe is made of one basic little thing. To make this complex and beautiful world, God reached into his parts bin and used one little thing over, and over again.

"Now consider the nonphysical universe. Your basic mystery forces of gravity, electromagnetics, and nuclear forces don't physically exist, but we know they are there. Interesting, isn't it? Something invisible without mass or form, but we can measure and observe their effects. The math to predict them is understood and predictable. God used one little thing plus a couple basic tools and wow!"

"I'll tell you what's curious," Steve interjected, "the invisible forces are the only thing holding the universe together. Everything we see held together by what we can't. But, what about heaven? What is it? What's dad got himself into?" Typical of Steve to up the ante on the question.

"Well, I was thinking. Consider human consciousness or maybe even our soul. It's the only difference between the moment from life to death. It's invisible, massless, and seems to not exist. But like the basic forces that hold the universe together, we know consciousness exists."

"Obvious, I suppose."

"Along with that come the associated layers of memory, emotions, and creative thoughts. You can make connections in the brain, but how is that a distinct memory, an invention, a composition, a plan? How does that make music, or love? I think our conscious thoughts are another intangible force in God's universe. Call it the life force.

"God made this universe from one basic thing. Incomprehensible complexity from one little thing. Imagine the heaven he made from billions of unique souls. Souls made up of life, memories, knowledge, and experience."

"That's good. I suppose every soul showing up in heaven is new material for God to work with." We paused again, taking in the slow satisfaction of an evening turning to dusk. "But there's just one thing I still wonder about."

"What's that?"

"Just what are these hills here for?"

ABOUT THE AUTHOR
G. Edward

Living on the Edge of Heaven

Over a career spanning more than thirty years, G. Edward has worked as an engineer, a technical salesman , a general manager, a consultant, and a business owner. While technical writing during his earliest years as an aerospace engineer, his creative prose caused both trouble and success. After a full corporate career, he moved on to start a hardware business. A connoisseur for people and experiences, real life is fertilizer for prose, and he returned to his love of a more creative style of writing. Writing feature columns for magazines and at Gedwardpress.com he writes “The Nuts and Bolts of Things”, “The Edge of Heaven”, and “Overheard at the Hardware Store.” He, his wife, and children gather at the shores of a lake in Wisconsin, just this side of heaven.

www.ingramcontent.com/pod-product-compliance
Lightning Source LLC
Chambersburg PA
CBHW071528040426
42452CB00008B/921

* 9 7 8 0 9 9 8 8 3 6 6 0 7 *